DARED

— TO BE ME THROUGH —

CANCER

Getting Crystal Clear on How to Fly

DARED
— TO BE ME THROUGH —
CANCER
Getting Crystal Clear on How to Fly

María Angélica Benavides, EdD, Publisher

Jorge Vásquez * Dr. Randi D. Ward * Diego Vásquez
Ewa Andrykiewicz Zmyslona * Helen Argyrou * Jeff Cade
Amelia Fjellvard * Dawn Gaden * Tamara L. Hunter * Dr. Wendy Labat
Dr. Michelle Mras * Laura Fernández Pérez * Coach MJ Tolan
Carlos René & the Ramírez Tribe

B-Global

B-Global

DEDICATION

We are dedicating this book to all those who have been affected by cancer especially survivors, families, and friends of lost ones. We pray this book brings some comfort, hope, and inspiration to help you find the light in the darkest moments of your lives. May you receive love and support and continue to be blessed in all you do! Live every day as if it is your last day!

In Loving
Memory

Francine Branch

10/16/1958 - 01/07/2023

A devoted, loving and caring mother.

My mother is the epitome of strength and courage. A true inspiration to me and so many others, she has shown me that anything is possible with the right attitude and hard work. It's her effortless grace, her unwavering optimism, and her unyielding love that I strive to embody every single day.

RIP Mom.

Your daughter Latina

In Loving
Memory

María Guadalupe Garza Méndez

01/28/1947 - 06/27/2022

4yr battle cancer!
MS.WONDER WOMEN !!

My mother was a fighter and courageous woman who never gave up. She was loving and a true inspiration to all who surrounded her. She was a devoted mother, grandmother, and true friend. I strive to embody her unconditional love. She will remain in our hearts forever!

Your daughter Andrea Garza

Children Name:
Jose Garza Mendez
Andrea Garza Mendez
Bernardo Garza Mendez. R.I.P
Xochilt Guadalupe Garza Mendez
Juan Carlos Garza Mendez

In Loving Memory

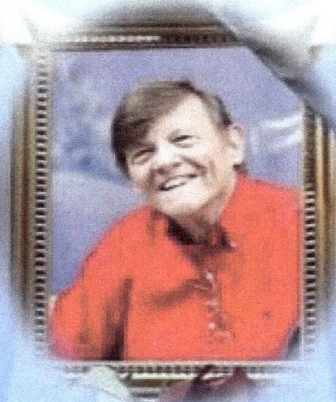

Billy D. Ward

Great Loving Husband and a Father

Billy D. Ward was my kind, supportive, loving husband for 48 years. He was a great father, best friend, and perfect mentor to our son Mark. We will never forget him, his humor, and his amazing ability to handle difficult situations. He was so special--- a one-of-a-kind!

ACKNOWLEDGEMENT

We would like to acknowledge all the Co-Authors who shared their heartfelt stories and inspiring messages in the book. We have no doubts that their stories will touch the lives of many.

We want to express our gratitude to Dr. Randi, our phenomenal editor devoted to making our chapters flow and ensuring the authors share their precise messages.

Thank you to Sharon Guiang for her dedication to formatting and designing the book images. She has been a blessing to work with and has done a remarkable job creating a magic touch to the flyers and promotional material. Thank you Sajjad Shehbaz for the beautiful book cover.

Dr. Angelica Benavides wants to acknowledge and thank her sons Jorge M. Vasquez and Diego Vasquez, sisters Lourdes Benavides and Blanca Jimenez, Leslie Mixon, Brian Louise, Norah Dykema, Sadie Shaw, Alice Linda Lambert Haney, Karen Wilks Boone, Angie Martinez, Veronica Rios, Pat Laing, Alma Rodrigues, Lety Rendon, Diana V., Garath, Patsy Sosa for being there for her throughout the most challenging moments of her life such spending hours in chemo, cooking and, ordering meals on wheels, taking her to doctor appointments, and most importantly lending her your shoulder to cry on. If you are not on this list and you supported me, Thank You for all you did for me. I am truly grateful. This list can be a whole book in itself. All of you are my sheroes and heroes!

The Other Co-Authors were given the opportunity to acknowledge people who were important to them and supported them.

ACKNOWLEDGEMENT

From Coach MJ Tolan

My mantra is 'I'M Possible' but I would never be 'possible' without the good Lord watching over me. A big shout out to my giant family and especially to my Terrific brothers, the Great 8, Patrick, Timothy, Shawn, Brian, Kevin, Martin, James.. Our Tribe is Tolan Strong, Tolan Brothers. Thanks to all who prayed for my recovery, let me tell you, prayers are heavenly emails and I appreciate every single one of them! Amen

From Ewa Andrykiewicz Zmyslona

"To my dear family and friends, who provided unwavering love and support throughout my journey with cancer, I cannot thank you enough. Your encouragement, laughter, and constant presence helped me find the strength to overcome adversity and heal. To my entire support team, including medical professionals, therapists, and fellow cancer friends, thank you for being a beacon of hope and for reminding me of the power of community."

From Jeff Cade

Thanking my Parents for their unconditional Love, guidance, & supportive Family members & Friends throughout my journey. Live, Love & be Well. My Parents names are Henry & Bess Cade: Loving Parents..gone too soon but never forgotten, who are in Spiritual essence with their Heavenly Creator & Ancestors!

From Tamara L.Hunter

"My family is my heart; those here and those who have gained their wings. My life was saved for you, dear reader. You can do this, we are here to support you. There is "Healing Through Connections.""

From Dr. Michelle Mras

Michael Mras, my husband, for your endless love, care and support throughout my sicknesses and our health. Mia and Matt Mras, our children, for stepping up in every aspect of your lives. Thank you for caring for me and Dad throughout this journey.

ACKNOWLEDGEMENT

From Amelia Fjellvard

To all those who have fought and continue to fight the battle against cancer, this chapter is dedicated to you. Your bravery and strength inspired me to share my own story, and I hope it brings comfort, hope, and inspiration to others. Thank you to my family and friends for their unwavering support and love during my journey. And to all the medical professionals who have cared for me, your expertise and compassion will always be appreciated. This chapter is a testament to the power of the human spirit and the importance of never giving up hope.

From Laura Fernández Pérez

I feel a deep and infinite gratitude for my dear teacher, friend and dear being, where, from the first moment I could feel his love through each word, each gesture and each glance, always enveloping me with his warm, strong and tender embrace at the same time. Thank you, thank you, thank you for yesterday, now and always, I love you Eduardo, thank you for being you and divine being.

All my love and gratitude to my dear Edna, who, even though she was far away, has been and is very close, always with her wisdom and genuine love, and her faith that everything would be fine, her strength and love always accompany me. Thank you, thank you, thank you my Edna, Wonder Woman, I love her.

From Dr. Wendy Labat

I'd like to acknowledge my husband, Carl, adult children, Erika, Craig, Cedric, and my sister Tanya for supporting me through my breast cancer journey. Most importantly I want to praise God for turning what could have been a tragedy into triumphant opportunities that have allowed me to empower others.

ACKNOWLEDGEMENT

From Carlos and Ramirez Tribe

To all those who knew and loved my mom, Raquel, we thank you for all the unconditional and continuous love and support. She appreciated all those who showed kindness, offered prayer and of course, laughter. She loved and appreciated every single one of you. As for the Ramirez Tribe, she's loved dearly, greatly missed and forever honored because of who she is for us all.

From Helen Argyrou

I want to thank my family, doctors, Ronald Van Naamen and friend Viola Edward for the care and support they gave me through my recovery.

As the Editor of this heartwarming Cancer Book, I, Dr. Randi D. Ward, would like to dedicate this book to two people: First, my beloved and wonderful husband Bill who died from lung cancer six days after it was diagnosed---a shocking, devastating death to my son and me with sadly no time to prepare for his death. Secondly, I want to express
my sincerest thanks, love, and appreciation to my friend and "sister" Dr. Angelica Benavides, a miraculous cancer survivor, for this incredibly powerful book which will
inspire and help so many people whose lives have been impacted by cancer.

***

TABLE OF CONTENTS

TABLE OF CONTENTS

FOREWORD

"You have CANCER" are words no one ever wants to hear, but sadly, too many people's lives have been affected by these three horrible words. Finding ways to remain positive and hopeful is a stressful, extremely difficult journey. The journey can end in a successful remission and/or cancer removal or tragically in death. The medical world's fight to find cures for the many forms of devastating cancer must continue. This book is one way in which this book's Co-Author/Publisher Angelica Benavides as a cancer survivor herself is providing hopeful messages from other cancer survivors or from families of those who lost their cancer battles. Profits from this book will also be donated to selected Cancer Programs specifically for children battling Cancer. Every dollar is important in this ongoing Campaign to eliminate Cancer in our world.

Every person in the world has been touched by Cancer in some way either personally or with a family member, friend, work associate, etc., so this book is designed to help and inspire everyone. Of course, these stories are not 100% happy. Cancer is an evil disease. The stories in this book discuss the lives of these amazing people before their cancer diagnoses, the types of cancer they had, the way their cancers were discovered, and their initial reactions to the disturbing news.

However, the authors also reveal the following beneficial things they did to remain positive:
1. advice on how they survived the "dark" days they faced;
2. their "Aha Moments", their lessons learned, and their achievements during their difficult times;
3. the courageous actions they are now taking;
4. their FOUR STEPS for other Cancer Patients to follow during their Cancer Journey;
5. their suggestions for self-love are desperately needed; and
6. the legacies they are now living as they do their best to help other cancer patients.

In addition, these incredible people share how family and friends supported them. Often family and friends are deeply confused and need genuine help and advice on how to deal with Cancer Patients or how to deal with the loss of a loved one effectively. The authors also recommend agencies and support organizations/communities that helped them on their journey.

As you read each story, you may feel sad, you may even shed a tear, but you will also smile and even laugh when you read the authors' humorous stories, their favorite quotes, and their final words of encouragement to cancer patients and to their families and friends. It was my honor to be the EDITOR of this remarkable book and to have worked closely with my dear friend Angelica Benavides.

It is our sincerest wish that this book will provide HOPE, LOVE, and INSPIRATION to all of you, readers. God bless all of you who are struggling with Cancer.

Dr. Randi D. Ward, Educator/Mentor, Best-Selling Author, Speaker, Book Coach, Master Editor, RM Infinite Co-Owner, Multi-Award Recipient - rminfinite1@gmail.com randiteach@yahoo.com
www.randidward.com; https://www.facebook.com/randi.ward

Dr. Randi D. Ward
Randi D. Ward, Author, Coach, Editor
Lawrenceville, Georgia, USA
randiteach@yahoo.com

Introduction

Life is like a roller coaster. We have our up moments and downs. We have happy moments and challenging moments. Life can be exciting and yet scary at the times. I have discovered life to be beautiful, adventurous, exciting, frustrating, crazy, difficult, and tough. I have learned to take the bull by its horns when it gets difficult and tough. I've learned to stay still during the toughest moments of life and just observe. I've learned to accept life as is and take responsibility for my experiences. I've learned to discover my life learnings.

I am writing this book and have asked other amazing people who have either experienced cancer or have lost a loved one to write a chapter. Our main goal is to inspire others going through tough times and/ or through cancer not to give up. Make every moment count! As you read the chapters, you might feel some sadness. Having cancer is not easy and losing the battle is much more difficult but we want you to start living life to the fullest. Don't wait for difficult moments to start turning your dreams into reality. I have discovered life is too short to waste time and energy on unnecessary things.

Stop! Reflect on what you truly desire. Discover what you need to achieve it. Do you need support, motivation, a skill, or training on how to get from A to Z? Find it and connect with all the amazing book collaborators in this book. They will help you one way or another. We are here to help you cross the bridge to dare to be you no matter what is happening in your life.

BIG Why—Creating a Mission to Millions

One of my greatest achievements in life is living! I was able to outlive two types of cancer. Before being diagnosed with cancer, I was doing Zumba and six inches of my intestines twisted; I nearly died at that time. During one of my surgeries in dealing with cancer, I ended up with a blood clot that led to a severe infection landing me in intensive care for more than a week. My greatest achievement and honor is being alive.

I realized I had a bigger mission to convince, inspire, and motivate women leaders around the world to live their life's purpose in a bigger way. During my most difficult times of life, I discovered **"Me"**. I realized that to achieve big dreams, you must take big risks. It is scary but Bravery is key. You must simply do it and take action towards your big dreams to achieve any success. Getting a message in front of millions might not be easy, but it is possible.

Create a mission for millions. Make sure to write a book that outlives you. Live and leave your message and story that are your golden nuggets on how you overcame challenges in life, s. So, our children, and future generations are inspired to keep going no matter how difficult life might seem. We need to encourage and inspire people to find love and joy within. We must celebrate small wins to motivate us and create momentum in our life. Remember to be present in all your life experiences. It is not the destination you seek but the experience of the journey that is brought to your soul. Collaborate and build strong relationships to have a sense of belonging and create supportive communities.

I stepped into my greatness when I found my voice, responsibility, and duty to the world that helps you and millions of women to share their Mission with Millions through my coaching programs, publishing books for entrepreneurs, my app, and B-Global masterminds, and business ventures. Visionary Leaders should strive toward optimal inclusion to create a strong community and strong connections, giving people a sense of belonging.

Tik Tok... TikTok! Time is ticking so go after what you truly desire. Don't allow anything to get in your way...not even cancer. Get crystal clear on what you want and go after it. Dare to Be YOU!

Chapter 1

A Time Daring to Be ME After Cancer

Dr.B

Dr. María Angelica Benavides

Ultimate Legacy Builder, A World-Class Storyteller, Serial Entrepreneur, and Publisher

Arlington, Tx - U.S.A

dr.angelica@drbglobal.net

I help women heal deep wounds of life by writing, publishing, and turning their mess into a message to inspire others around the world.

> **"** ———
>
> *It doesn't matter how many times you fall. What matters is that you learn to bounce right back and learn to laugh along the way.*
>
> *Angelica Benavides (Dr. B)*

Dr. Angelica Benavides is known as Dr. B. and the Ultimate Legacy Builder. She increases visibility, exposure, and influence, helping entrepreneurs be all they can be. Dr. B's [Angélica Benavides (Underwood) Ed.D.] story is being written and shared worldwide by the Women's World Conference and Awards. She has been featured on NBC, USA Today, and Fox and recognized as an Amazing Woman of Influence. She shared a Global Virtual Stage with Forbes Riley, Bill Walsh, Ragne Sinikas, and Dr. Freddy Behin. Dr. B. received Lady of All Nations award, 100 Most Successful Women award, and SuperHero Award.

Dr. B. shows women entrepreneurs how to scale their businesses. She teaches them how to become financially literate and how to use financial knowledge to make better decisions from everyday spending to long-term financial planning. Throughout the chapter in bold words, Dr. B. will share her key recipes to help you share your Mission with Millions.

Confidence Keeps Us From Our Dreams
Believe it or not, I was a very shy young girl and lacked confidence when growing up. I have always liked challenges in life even before cancer. However, the lack of confidence kept me far from my dreams. I remember trying out for the Golden Spurs (cheerleader) in high school. I joined the choir in church and wanted to sing with a band. (Honestly, I had no voice so your ears must be happy I didn't keep singing—jejeje). Once I achieved something I usually gave it up right away; my lack of confidence always made me doubt myself. I would achieve things and then let go of what I desired. I had a silly belief that I needed to be perfect at the time of wanting and achieving something. What I have come to realize is that perfection is the action or process of improving something; however, I believed that perfection was a quality of being free from all flaws which meant that it wasn't me or ever ready to achieve anything.

A Time Daring to Be ME After Cancer

You might also be feeling or believing the same thing. If so, you will not be perfect at the time, but remember perfection is a process and ongoing. Go after what you want and desire!

Bad News Can Numb You But Doesn't Hold You Back

I always thought cancer happens to others. Hard to say and awful beliefs, right? I know… Let's say it only happens in the movies. One day, reality hit me. I was told that I had cancer. At that moment, my world froze, and I felt nothing. It was as if I was numb or didn't know what to feel or think at the time.

Maybe, just maybe, my dreams and unconscious mind prepared me for the day I was told I had cancer. Before being told I had cancer, I had a strange dream. I dreamed a man gave me a dog. The man said, "Here is your Reiki dog." I said, "My Reiki dog." Hmmm... A week later a lady who rescues dogs told my son who was working at Office Max that she had a dog and was looking for someone to adopt the dog. We went to see Archie the dog that we immediately fell in love with. You are probably wondering… a dog? What does this have to do with my cancer story? Well, my Archie had cancer. It spread through his whole body really fast. He had surgery, and when we brought him home from surgery, it dawned on me about my dream about my Reiki dog. I told my son about this dream as I was walking into the house with the dog and said, "What the fudge? I think I have cancer." I had no symptoms, just a feeling that something was wrong. I went to get checked and received the unfortunate news. I didn't allow this news to hold me back. I started to make my dreams reality. Stop dreaming but start living your dreams!

Make Every Moment Count Even in Dark Moments

Everyone at one time or another will experience the Dark Night of the Soul. It is through those dark moments that we gain the courage and confidence to find the exit of what we might consider the failure freeway. Just like every storm shall pass — all challenges and dark moments will pass. I lived through almost 7 years of intense challenges. My whole life tumbled right in front of me. I experienced everything all at once. I was diagnosed with two types of cancer and was faced with divorce, bankruptcy, and foreclosure. These were the darkest moments of my life. My boys and I had to figure things out and learn how to play the game of life to survive, heal, and find the way out of this darkness. Most importantly, I learned to live and make every moment count! Now, I am living and leaving a legacy for generations to come.

Heal Your Life's Journey

My healing journey was long and challenging. One thing I discovered during these dark times was to "turn my mess into a message" to encourage and inspire other women to keep going no matter how hard life seems. I gained the courage and bravery to step into the best version of myself. Every obstacle becomes a lesson and opportunity to grow and transform in every aspect of my life. I have gained the belief that " I am enough" to do, achieve, and inspire other to do the impossible. That is achieve bigger goals!

I am now helping women spread their message through storytelling and delivering the right message to the right audience. I inspire and motivate women entrepreneurs to write books that outlive them and help them heal through writing and align to their best version of who they are and who they need to become to achieve the bigger version of themselves. I am supercharging women business owners to take big ideas into reality and help them step into their greatness.

I help women clarify and establish a mission to be delivered to millions of people around the world to raise awareness, empower people into leadership, and elevate them to serve people around the world. A visionary woman leader must take responsibility to create a mission and legacies that will take our future generations to places we never imagined we could reach.

A Time Daring to Be ME After Cancer

One of my giant steps was connecting with women around the world and encouraging them to turn their mess into a message by writing and publishing a book to share their message with millions. Innovation is

another recipe for spreading your Mission to Millions. Use the internet, get on podcasts, or create your own; use online TV such as Apple TV or Amazon Fire TV. If it doesn't exist, invent it. You have a greater being within you that has the confidence and power to achieve your big dreams. I believe in you. You should believe in yourself, too! Believing in yourself is a vital key you must use and use again in your Million to Millions journey because if you don't, no one else will.

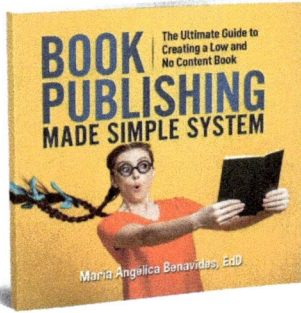

My Business Were Born From Times Of Uncertainty

My business was born in times of uncertainty. I was living a life that defies the odds. I am the ninth of eleven children born to Mexican immigrants. I struggled in the English (monolingual) classroom and often doubted my ability to succeed. As a native Spanish speaker, I struggled in all classes - especially reading. I was the first in my family to finish high school, but even on my graduation, I wondered. "How did that happen?" After finishing high school, I took menial jobs that did not require much education. I felt that, despite my diploma, I probably would not amount to much. Fortunately, one of my employers saw what I did not see in myself: potential. Armed with confidence, I enrolled in Laredo Community College and earned a doctoral degree in Leadership and Specialized in Curriculum. I have proven that success is possible for everyone by creating a plan and sticking to it through thick and thin!

I have gained the unique ability to help people release the mental obstacles that prevent them from achieving their very best at work, in business, and in life. I am committed to empowering others to exchange the chaos of life for the best life possible. I help people unlock their full potential and believe their time is now. I share my personal story of how I beat cancer and how to heal your body and your life. I share some of my challenges in life and how I overcame the darkest moments of my life, turning them into light, joy, love, and empowerment.

A Time Daring to Be ME After Cancer

I am committed to providing a RoadMap to my online coaching platform. I connect with other passionate women and unique voices who share their challenges and how they overcame life challenges. I empower women in all areas of life, such as health, money, relationships, education, and career by teaching them universal laws and how to play the game of life. Life is simply a game you must learn how to play to achieve your highest potential and live on purpose to be self-actualized.

World Travel Courage and Legacy Building

Another courageous action I am now taking that I wouldn't have taken before cancer is becoming a world traveler. I am having the most amazing moments of my life. A special friend recently told me "anything worth doing, is worth doing right." Hunter S Thompson. Not only doing it right but actually doing what you truly desire. You see I realized that I had broken promises I had made to myself. For years, I had wanted to travel the world but always had excuses such as I don't have time, don't have enough money, or none of my friends' schedules didn't align with mine. I finally made a decision to just do it. I started traveling with or without a friend. The most remarkable thing is that I have made amazing friends around the world. I have found not only friends but joy, laughter, and adventure. Do what you desire without regrets! I have become a world traveler, living, and leaving a legacy.

4 steps Playing the Game of Life

I highly recommend 4 steps for people battling cancer to play the game of life. I strongly recommend the following:

1. Tap into your passion.
2. Turn your dreams into reality.
3. Make every moment count.
4. Find happiness in everything you do.

A Time Daring to Be ME After Cancer

Look if you live for a day or more. Live as if it is your last day.

As I mentioned above, I had broken promises before cancer. I had many promises that I would do and achieve but everyone was on hold for the perfect day to do it. You must **Dare** to do the things you have never done before, especially what you desire to do!

I traveled to Thailand and saw a beautiful white tiger and decided to pet it. I was so frightened like many other things in life but stepped into bravery and courage. I had to breathe deeply and walk calmly toward the white tiger. I also got to hold a snake that freakin' scared me. I hiked for 5-days in Peru not long after radiation and chemo. I kept asking the tour guide to get a

helicopter to come to get me. (smiles). He said he couldn't do that but encouraged me to take ten steps and stop and raise my arms and breathe. Believe it or not, I have had to do these same strategies over and over again in times of fear and doubt. but I don't let anything stop me from living and experiencing the joy of doing.

My sons were young. Jorge was 17 years old, and Diego was 10 years old. They struggled with me emotionally, and yet they also stepped into bravery and courage during these dark moments. What I remember the most was when my hair was dry as corn hulks. My son woke me up around 1 a.m. My oldest son Jorge said, "Mom, it is time."

I said, "Time for what?"

He said, "To bald your hair." Gosh, I cried like a baby. My hair felt like my superpowers were being taken away. Even more, when I had to decide if I would have a double mastectomy, it was another difficult decision to make. My oldest said, "Mom if you don't try everything to live I will be so mad."

A Time Daring to Be ME After Cancer

It was a hard decision, but I do everything for my kids. My youngest found a YouTube video by a Dr. Michael Salzhauer a plastic surgeon, known as Dr. Miami who films his surgeries. He did the research for me to encourage me and help me make an informed decision. What I realized is that doctors have been given divine light and guidance on how to help millions to not only heal but to receive reconstruction that is beyond normal. It is a gift from God. I call it the Art of the Healer. These doctors not only heal us but help us tap into feeling "normal" again. I had to take it a step further by tapping into feeling sexy after cancer. Stay tuned to my new book coming soon "

Outside Support
No one should cope with cancer without support. I had remarkable support from many people around me. I did have to learn to ask for help and accept the help. It was another difficult thing for me to do because for years I thought I could do things on my own. I have to admit that I was wrong.

My sisters Blanca Jimenez and Lourdes Benavides were with me encouraging me, supporting me, and helping me in every way they could. I am so grateful for them. This meant the world to me.
My co-workers offered me help in so many ways. They took turns taking me to my doctor's appointments. They also sent me meals on wheels. They were very attentive to ensure that my needs were met.

Cancer Care Services offers financial, emotional, and educational resources during this cancer journey. They help and provide hope to people battling cancer in our community. There was one Christmas that I had no energy or money to buy Christmas gifts — to my surprise a couple knocked at my door. They brought many gifts that filled up my whole dining room with Christmas presents. My eyes teared up, and now I am paying it forward to children battling cancer. I highly recommend this service. https://cancercareservices.org/mission-history/

A Time Daring to Be ME After Cancer

Every year for the past four years, I have had a toy drive. This year I joined forces with Francesca and Diana, and together we gathered more than 300+. My goal is to double this number every year. My heart is supporting orphans and children around the world.

Outliving Life Circumstances is a Success

All women need to inspire other women to do everything in their power to thrive in life and leave a legacy. You see leaving a legacy is more than giving an inheritance and trust ... a generational legacy is leaving ideas, stories, perspectives, and/or beliefs that are emotionally or culturally passed down from our families to the world. A legacy is an opportunity to change the world. It is an opportunity to live for a purpose bigger than yourself and bless those around you.

I stepped into my greatness when I found my voice, responsibility, and duty to the world that helps you and millions of women to share their Mission with Millions through my coaching programs, publishing books for entrepreneurs, my app, and B-Global masterminds, and business ventures. Visionary Leaders should strive toward optimal inclusion to create a strong community and strong connections, giving people a sense of belonging.

Convinced that people have the power to reach their own potential, I know everyone has a story to tell that will transform people's lives around the world who are waiting to hear your story. Today more than ever the world awaits you and is looking for the job, products, or services that you can create. It is time to start your business or reinvent how your business operates. The truth is that your business is not unique; the reality is that **you are unique**. You need to leave a legacy that outlives you by telling your story and sharing your message with the world.

> *Live life even if it seems small. One day you will look back and see that it is bigger than it seemed.*
>
> *Angelica Benavides (Dr. B)*

Free Gift

I help entrepreneurs find that story and tell it to the world by writing a book and creating your signature talk to help you overcome the wounds of the past.

Telling your story can be cathartic and make you grow as a person, give you satisfaction, and allow you to increase your chances of success. It takes you out of that dark area that perhaps you thought ruined your life forever. It shows you the light. Share your light with others who are waiting for your life-transforming message. You will leave this experience with a feeling of dominance. Connect with me—-I coach you to bring out the book that have been burning inside you to be birthed! I am a Content Author Coach! Write a book, publish it, get on stages, and give hope to those waiting for your light to shine!

You are here to make a big difference in the world. The best way to do this is to use your story, experience, knowledge, and advice to help others be successful. This strategy that I share with you will guide you in a process so that through your story you can package and share advice, systems, tools, and processes, and create a lucrative business that impacts lives. Plus, leave a legacy that outlives you!

Get my free **4-Online Video Series** below called Book Publishing Made Simple System so you can get started with writing your book or start with a low-content book that is a notebook or journal.

Learn more about this author

Venture With Dr. B.

Accolades

My certifications are Associate in Arts, Bachelor of Interdisciplinary, Master of Science, and Doctoral Leadership with a Specialization in Curriculum & Instruction. These don't define me but shape who I am now. I have always been curious about Learning Theories, Human Development, and how the brain functions. I am dedicated a decade to researching and discovering how humans learn, develop, and how we can shift our beliefs to shift our decision-making and actions.

I have learned from the giants such as Anthony Robbins, Dean Graziosi, John Maxwell, Grant Cardone, Forbes Riley, Bill Walsh, and Mark Victor Hansen to help me think bigger, make bigger decisions, and take giant action steps toward my mission to millions. I now create even more success for business women owners. I specialize in publishing books, business programs, speaker training programs, certification programs, and global masterminds. I put on the table the best resources that every business needs to learn about to survive and thrive in any economy. My message has been delivered as cutting-edge content.

I am known as Dr. B. I inspire women worldwide to share their Mission with Millions and their stories. I am a Badass Influencer, an Ultimate Legacy Builder, A World-Class Storyteller, Best-Selling Author, Serial Entrepreneur, and Publisher.

I am a Marketing Director, Advisory Board Member, and Publisher for the Face of Women of Heart Awards (WOHA) for 2021. I was recently invited to the International Advisory Board for the 100 Successful Women in Business Network.

***

Chapter 2

Achieve Mind Over Matter

David Diego E. Vasques

David Diego E Vasquez

Brazilian Jiu-Jitsu Purple Belt

Arlington, Tx, USA
dvasquezbjj@gmail.com

Achieve Mind Over Matter

Diego Vasquez is a Brazilian Jiu-Jitsu purple belt. As a 17-year-old, Diego won the first adult male World Champion under Daniel Alvarez. He is a two-time Submission Hunter Pro Super Fight Winner and multiple-time IBJJF gold medalist. He won third place and the Pan American Championship. Sports has always been his passion, and he uses sports to help him relieve stress, anxiety, and other emotions. Jiu-Jitsu has helped him accomplish many things off and on the mat. He is the founder of the 50/50 Fitness Lockdown Virtual Challenge. Diego is a co-author 0f "De Cero al Éxito" book and the author of the Jiu-Jitsu Notebook. My mom is Dr. Angelica Benavides known as the Ultimate Legacy Builder and world traveler. You will read her chapter in this book as well.

Freak Accident and the Nightmare Began

Everything changed one day. Everything seemed normal before the big news. One never knows what will happen in life so live every day to the fullest. I was in middle school when my mom was diagnosed with cancer.

I was passionate about football and was a football player. My mom was dropping me off at one of my games. I noticed she felt sick and was throwing up on the way to my game. She dropped me off, and the next thing I knew she was hospitalized. That whole day, I went without eating and ended up at the hospital with my mom. I felt the day go by slowly as if my world had stopped. My mom was at Zumba when a freak accident happened to her. Almost a year before my mom was diagnosed with cancer, she went to the doctor

on November 10, 2012; she had surgery to remove 6 inches of her intestine. Her intestines twisted, and she nearly died, and the nightmare began. I even feel that I lost part of myself during that time. The next year she was diagnosed with two types of cancer. We moved out of our home. I had to move to a different school district which I hated and was miserable. I stopped being part of the football team. It took me a couple of years to find myself again. Yet, I feel I am now more consciously aware of my inner feelings, wants, and needs.

Achieve Mind Over Matter

Gaining Strength From Bad News

My mom took it a lot better than I did. I didn't know anything was going on. I couldn't see anything suspicious. My mom is always having events to inspire entrepreneurs. One day, we were going around to different hotels to find a venue because my mom was hosting a conference. And we stopped at a venue and before we went inside, she just told me that I went to the doctor, and they told me I have cancer. I just started to break down and cry. She just told me everything's 'gonna be fine' and to not worry. We just shook it off as if nothing happened and went into the hotel. It was hard news, but it made us stronger.

My mom has always been a superhero to me, and I never wanted to leave her side. I'm a momma's boy forever, and wherever she went, so did I, whether it was helping her at work or setting things up for her events or traveling to different states to see amazing gurus like Tony Robbins who lifted our spirits and helped us break through our limiting beliefs and emotions not serving us. I even participate on stage with her to motivate and inspire others to keep moving forward. Don't give up! Find a coach or guru to lift you up. Connect with us. We are here to support you through this journey.

Finding Your Inner Beauty — Dr. Angelica Benavides — Mari Strong FOUNDATION

Achieve Mind Over Matter

Fake It Until You Make it

I discovered my big why during dark moments. I found a new passion, Jiu Jitsu, which keeps me in a championship mindset. Sometimes, you will feel numb and not like yourself. I had to be strong for my mom and shut down my emotions for her. Is this the right thing to do? Maybe not! She was going through so much more than health issues as you will read in her chapter. Life is not easy. There is always someone out there struggling or going through a more difficult time than you. Jiu Jitsu kept me going so I could release my stress. You know, whether it's your kids, your spouse, your parents or brothers, sisters, or friends, just know there's a bigger reason why we go through these tough moments and just keep moving forward even if we fail forward. Find something you are passionate about and do it.

Sometimes, we need to fake it until we make it. You know, we're not going to know the words to say; we don't know if it's going to help or hurt the person we are trying to console. One day, I broke down and couldn't pretend anymore. My mom had internal bleeding and was in intensive care. She was going to have surgery for "the millionth time". Yes, I am exaggerating, but she had been in and out of the hospital multiple times. I burst into tears just before my mom went into surgery. I called her and cried my eyes out. My mom had to tell me to calm down. She said everything was going to be okay. She needed me to be strong, especially now that she was going into surgery.

You know your loved ones need you to be strong for them. I would spend hours in chemo with her. It was hard but I wanted to do it. I handled each event or difficult moment in many different ways. All I want to say is if you want to cry, Cry! If you want to scream,

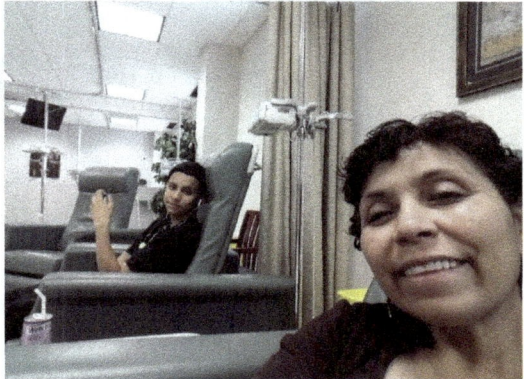

Scream! The only thing I have to say is that I think I put on an act in front of my mom most of the time and with my brother. Then when I was at school or by myself, I would be angry and upset and feel confused. I felt lost and didn't know what to do, especially when my mom was giving up at times.

Achieve Mind Over Matter

One time said she didn't want to live anymore. I would think about that all the time. I think my mom said it because she was tired of fighting the battle. She went through a double mastectomy and lost body parts that made her feel less sexy. She lost her breast and her hair which led to her losing her confidence and the feeling of being beautiful.

I have to say, it's okay to ask for help. Talk to your counselors, your siblings, and your parents. Find a coach and just ask for help. I am now offering Neuro-Linguistic Programming coaching sessions to help others break through their limiting beliefs and emotions. It helps me during difficult times. It will help you, too!

Try, Try All You Can, and Live

My mom tried so many things during her healing journey. Some things were crazy and unusual treatments. Now, we laugh about some of those treatments and faces she would make while trying them. My mom was highly motivated to heal. One time she took something called "gorgojos" in Spanish not sure if they are weevils, but they are said to improve the immune system. Did it work? Not sure but the point is she tried everything she heard about. The other crazy thing she did was Cold Cap Therapy during chemotherapy. It freezes hair follicles, and the scalp needs to get cold to -22 degrees Fahrenheit. My mom said, "It felt like an ice cream headache." Man, we would put it on her.

She would crunch up with a warm blanket and just take the coldness of the caps. We would wait there with her during chemo.

Every twenty-five minutes we changed the cap during the entire chemo treatment. My brother Jorge and I ended up balding my mom's hair which I might say trying different treatments gave her control over her well-being and gave us a sense of feeling she was not giving up. I gave her my spiderman beaning cap that she wore all the time.

Achieve Mind Over Matter

I also had to learn to drive at a very young age (14 years old) to take her to chemo and doctor appointments. Now, this is a hilarious story to tell. My mom taught me how to drive, but I started driving only half a block, and she would immediately tell me

to stop. She would shut her eyes which got me nervous, too. I remember my mom going crazy. She would make me ride the brake. She would tell me to stop when a car was behind and would tell me to let them pass me. I wasn't allowed to make turns at the beginning. It was nerve-wracking, but now we laugh about this. My brother Jorge ended up teaching me, too. Then all of a sudden, my mom let me drive all the way to Kroger on my own. One of the times my mom was in the hospital my aunt gave me the keys to her van to drive on the highway. My mom freaked out when she found out, but we all laughed.

I was motivated to do research to help my mom at 14 years of age. I started looking on YouTube before her double mastectomy to see what it was and if this would be a good decision for her. I found a YouTube video from Dr. Miami who was educating women via Youtube on different procedures. Dr. Miami was getting really big around that time, and he was doing breast reconstructions. Everything, you name it—tummy tucks, nipple reconstructions, and boob augmentations. You name it!

Being a young teenager telling my mom about this type of treatment was weird, but it helped me open up in so many ways with my mom. I said to my mom, "Hey, go, get a double mastectomy and whatever else that you need to do." My mom took my advice and encouragement. She is still here with us, and I can talk to her about anything in life.

I told my mom she would be okay if she did the surgery. YouTube helped her regain a new perspective and confidence and make a decision to get off the exit of those dark moments she was going through not knowing what to do or not. She decided to go through a double mastectomy. I am not saying you or your loved one should do this, but this was something my mom decided to do. My brother and I supported her 100% along the way.

Achieve Mind Over Matter

Now, you go find all types of treatment that might or might not work for you. You won't know until you try it. If it works, hooray! If it doesn't, you gain experience, and hey, you might end up laughing as we do now with some of the crazy treatments she tried.

Try everything. Try everything possible. Don't take the easy way out. My mom always tells me we have to be a better version of ourselves, and we're not lazy. We don't give up. We just keep moving forward.

My Mom Is My Superwoman
Every challenge brings an "Aha Moment". You learn something, and it should make you stronger. I am a Jiu-Jitsu trainer and coach now. Grappling and competing is a challenge. I don't always win, but I gain knowledge on the dos and don'ts of life.

I'm still healing today. I experienced many things during this journey and life itself. I hid a lot of my emotions and pushed them down inside because I felt I had to be strong for my mom. I don't really remember communicating about things that scared me. There are some things I didn't want to know and didn't want to learn. I was in shock. But whatever emotions I did have I just really kept them to myself. There were only a few people who could relate, and it was just us three; that is my mom, brother, and me.

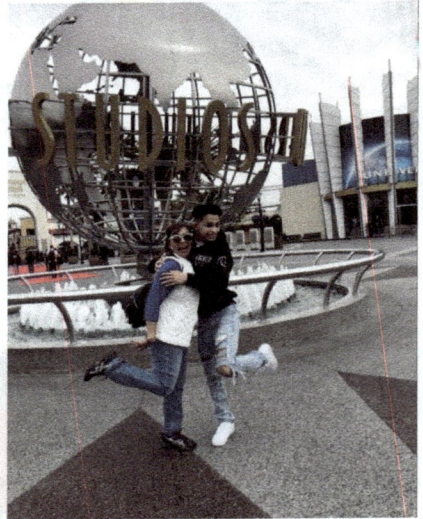

We all became superheroes in our own way. We all brought some motivation, inspiration, or information to my mom. All three of us learned so many things along the way such as treatments my mom would take, and we all gained bravery and courage.

What I have learned now as I reflect back in time—is that I didn't communicate as well as I should have. It's okay to cry. It's okay to let your loved ones who are diagnosed with cancer know how you feel because we are all in this together. Let your loved one know how you feel because it's also your journey. This is going to affect you for the rest of your life, no matter what the outcome is. So make sure you get help and support. Be there for your loved ones. Communicate—communication is key.

Take Control of Your Life

Number one is breathing. Your breathing controls how you feel. It controls your emotions. So really try to control your breathing. Number two, don't go off impulse. Impulse can help, but you can make a wrong decision of impulse. Research information to find the best treatment. Take control of yourself so watch what you eat and put into your body.

Because what you put into it is what you're gonna get. Finally, tell your family you love them every day so you live with no regrets. I tell my mom I love her all the time.

There is only one of YOU.

There is only one of us. How you treat yourself is how you want others to treat you. Give yourself positive affirmations. Say things like: I'm a nice person. I am beautiful. I am a loving person. My mom wrote, "I am enough." She had those words all over the house. Make sure to always have a smile and be kind to others. It will increase dopamine in your body which are the happy hormones that you need to strengthen your immune system. Most importantly, find your passion and don't let anyone tell you what you can and can't do.

No one can control your life except for you.

Live your passion. My mom is a world traveler now. I didn't want to travel at first until just recently. She travels all over the world. She has gone to Thailand, Ireland, Spain, and many other places. So I'm like I want to travel, and I want to do it with her.

Achieve Mind Over Matter

Do what makes you happy! We both like to enjoy life as much as we can. We have weird moments.

Go-Go, Mom and Everyone Going Through Cancer!

My aunts Blanca and Lourdes were there for us during those difficult moments. I learned who's really there for me and my mom and my family. The people who care about us have always supported us since then. I'm just forever grateful for everyone who helped out even prior to my mom having cancer. My mom had a special friend whom we will love forever and who supported her spiritually; that is Gareth. I shaved my hair to give her courage. Plus, I added my cowboy design to make it fun.

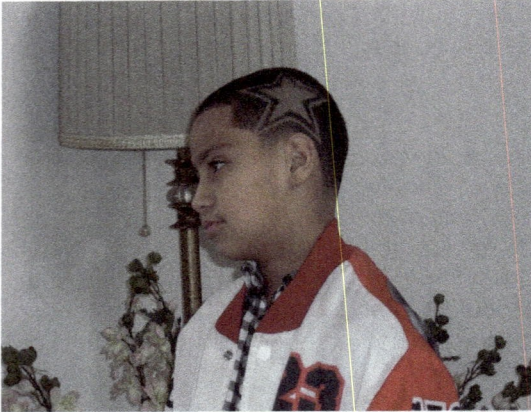

My mom never stopped supporting me and my dreams even through her challenges. She is always there for me. She would drop by and would always be there at my games. She cheers the loudest for both teams. I can still hear the sound of the cowbell that she would ring and scream my name, "Go Diego–Go"! Now, I cheer you on, "Go–Go! You have got what it takes to make it!"

Pay It Forward With Gifts and Love

My mom received help from Cancer Care Services agency in Fort Worth, Texas. I remember one Christmas a family brought us so many gifts that it filled our whole dining room. We were not expecting gifts this Christmas because my mom was too sick to go to the store. You know we were fine with not getting gifts because my mom was alive. These were the best presents we could have. It was amazing to watch and witness that these people didn't even know us and gave us a memorable Christmas for which we are forever grateful.

Achieve Mind Over Matter

Now we're giving donations to children who have cancer every Christmas. We do a toy drive to pay it forward. Go out and make a contribution to touch hearts and bring a smile to someone's face.

Nothing Can Stop You—Only You

I believe my mom will be a saint one day. She gives so much to humanity, loves everyone, and has a kind heart. I also know she will be a multimillionaire entrepreneur who will be helping kids all around the world whether it's going to Africa, Mexico, or India. She is always focused on educating children or building wells for water for children in poverty. She is also focused on helping students with disabilities.

She has helped several of my friends by giving them advice and giving them a place to stay. She has helped raise her nephew and nieces; you name it. All her nephews and nieces look up to her in so many ways. She is leaving a long-lasting legacy. When she is gone, she is leaving a mark on this world and people's hearts that will be passed down from generation to generation. I also want to change the world and help people like my mom. I want to continue to be a World Champion in Jiu Jitsu. My mom and I wake up saying to each other "10X, 10X" meaning let's double

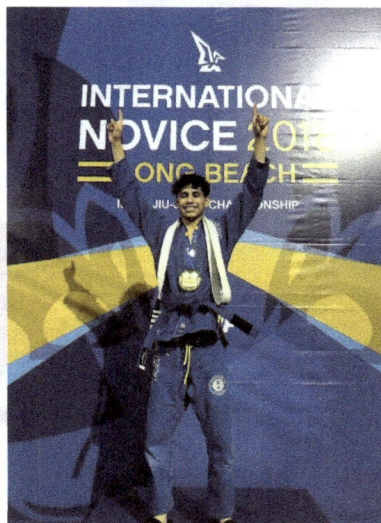

our efforts and just do it! Achieve anything and everything we want in life. We are now authors sharing our stories and messages to the world to inspire others to go after their dreams and to motivate them to never give up!

Achieve Mind Over Matter

Nothing can stop you, only you. You're not alone. Keep fighting the fight. Go on Facebook. Find groups and communities who have been through the same things because it's going to help you.

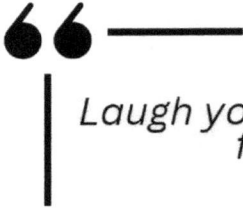

" —

Laugh your heart out daily to create the feel-good daily dosage.

Diego Vasquez

Let's Connect on Social Media

Get Our Notebook to brainstorm and reflect

Chapter 3

Cure Your Financial ills

Dr. Wendy Labat

Dr. Wendy Labat

The Financial Healer

Fayettevile, GA USA

drwendylabat@thefinancialcures.com

> **❝** ————
> *When you think right, speak right, and do right, things will flow right to optimize your financial health.*
>
> *—Dr. Wendy Labat*

Dr. Wendy Labat, The Financial Healer empowers entrepreneurs, executives, and individuals to overcome anorexic income, obese debt, mindset and knowledge deficiency, spending addiction, and other financial ills to take control over their finances, acquire proper protection, build a financial legacy, enjoy financial freedom, and live the life they desire.

Using Laughter as Your Medicine
After my first chemotherapy infusion, I asked my daughter to wash my hair. After she rinsed out the shampoo, my hair was so matted, I told her to shave my head instead of trying to comb through the mess. It was so funny to see my hair look like a sheep's ass (excuse my language). Laugh at yourself even when you don't feel like it.

Dr. Wendy Labat, The Financial Healer, is the CEO of The Financial Cures LLC, an MWBE. She created **The Financial Cures System**®, a results-based program for financial mastery. Dr. Labat is the best-selling author of **The Financial Cures Book Series**: **Diagnose Your Financial Health** and **Optimize Your Financial Health.** She is the producer and host of the award-winning global streaming production of **Financial Cures with Dr. Wendy Labat,** an award-winning entrepreneur, business strategist, and international speaker.

Happy, Healthy, and Successful.

In March 2017, I was notified that the results of my semi-annual mammogram required a biopsy to test a growth that showed up on the image. A couple of days later I underwent the biopsy and was told the results would be back in about 3 days. I called the radiology department 3 days later only to be told I would get the results from my doctor.

When I called my doctor's office, I was told that I would have to schedule an appointment. I told her to schedule an appointment. The receptionist put me on hold for about 3 minutes. The office manager got on the line and told me that the doctor does not make appointments to discuss test results. I would have to come in to pick them up.

I immediately drove to the doctor's office. When I arrived, I was handed a sealed envelope with the test results. I sat in my car, opened the envelope, and read the results. I saw the word "carcinoma" and knew I had breast cancer. God turns lemons into lemonade. I did not cry or panic.

A sense of peace came over me. I had no clue where to go from there, so I called a friend who was a breast cancer conqueror. She gave me her doctor's phone number. I called her doctor's office, explained the situation, and was told to fax my biopsy results to his office. Within 5 minutes of faxing the results, I received a callback. I gave the person on the phone my information. She told me that they did not accept my insurance but said she would call me right back. About 10 minutes later, she called back and gave me the number to The Winship Cancer Institute at Emory University. She told me to call them right away because they were waiting for my call. Sure enough, they took my information and scheduled an appointment for me to see an oncologist 3 days later. In the meantime, I did all kinds of research about breast cancer. I did not know anything about the disease other than what I had seen on TV commercials for various breast cancer drugs. Nobody in my family had breast cancer.

Cure Your Financial ills

I asked my breast cancer conqueror friend to tell me about her experience. Not only did she share her experience with me, but she also showed me the scars from her botched reconstructive surgeries. I researched the facility, types of chemotherapy, types of cancer, and the surgical options available. I wanted to be prepared for my appointment with the oncologist so I could ask questions and make informed decisions about my course of treatment for the disease.

I met with my oncologist. She thoroughly explained the results of my biopsy stating that I had HER2+ breast cancer. She explained that it is a very aggressive form of cancer and explained my treatment options. I chose the most aggressive form of treatment.

Trust God and His Word Every Day. Praise Him Even When Your Life is Tumbling Down.
Trust God and His word. Pray and confess His word about healing. Continually praise Him and show gratitude. Get a prayer team of people you trust who are prayer warriors. Stay positive no matter how bad things look. Don't let negative people or energy into your space. Know that everything happens for the good no matter how bad it looks.

My healing journey began when I felt a sense of peace come over me as I read my biopsy results while sitting in my car outside the doctor's office. I knew it wasn't a death sentence, but I also knew it wasn't going to be an easy journey.

That's when I decided to put my trust and faith in God to see me through. I didn't know what to do next or where to go to seek treatment. One thing I did know was that I could not depend on the doctor who refused to give me the results of my biopsy. I asked God to order my steps, and He did. From that moment on I depended on The Spirit to guide me through my breast cancer journey.

I did not make a decision or take any action about my treatment until I got confirmation from God. My chemo treatments and surgeries took a toll on my body and mind. I was in the final stages of completing my doctoral degree. I was determined to finish and walk across the stage to be hooded as Dr. Wendy Labat. I stayed positive and prayed up, especially when I didn't have the strength or motivation. God always makes a way and carries you through.

Aha Moments
I created *The Financial Cures System*®, a results-based program to teach financial mastery after winning my battle with breast cancer. The program provides vital information, tools, and resources that empower entrepreneurs, executives, families, and individuals to overcome anorexic income, obese debt, mindset/knowledge deficiencies, and other financial ills to take control over their finances, acquire proper protection to prevent financial ruin, build a financial legacy, create generational wealth, become financially free, and live the life they desire.

Cure Your Financial ills

Breast cancer is being conquered every day. Don't let the cancer diagnosis cause you to think the worst. Look forward to sharing your story as encouragement for others to get through their journey.

There are four things in which I am a firm believer:
1) Pray for healing
2) Stay positive and thankful
3) Laugh as much as possible
4) Cry when you need to.

I don't have broken promises that needed mending. When things don't go as planned, I know something better is coming. God closes one door because a better door is waiting for you to open and go through.

Keep Filling Your Cup
Life's lessons have taught me that you can't pour from an empty cup. Your body may be tired, but your mind can help rejuvenate it. Listen to or read daily inspirations. Take care of yourself first. Do whatever makes you happy. Enjoy "me time" regularly. In the beginning, I was able to continue my regular self-care activities like getting my hair and nails done, going shopping, eating out, and stay hydrated.

Family Follows Your Lead
My husband was the first person I called after reading the biopsy results. I waited until I got home to tell the other members of my family. My daughter and youngest son cried but were relieved when I assured them that my cancer diagnosis was not a death sentence. My husband, and sister reacted pretty well because I am a very positive and spiritual person.

Cure Your Financial ills

God gave me a sense of peace about the diagnosis so I knew things were going to be alright. I didn't kid myself by thinking that the journey was going to be easy, but I did know that I had to have the right mindset to get me through the difficult times.

I had a small group of prayer warriors that prayed on my behalf daily. It was a mix of close family, friends, acquaintances, and clients. I didn't share my diagnosis with many people because I didn't want any pity parties. God identified who would be part of this group.

I found myself speaking with strangers about my situation only to find that breast cancer impacted them personally or a member of their family. I realized that breast cancer was more prevalent than I ever imagined. I was relieved to see how positive and vibrant these breast cancer conquerors were.

Get Your Affairs In Order

My cancer diagnosis turned into a crusade to empower others to prevent financial ruin from an illness or injury. My immediate family is my support system. This was also a wake-up call for me to get our family affairs up to date and in order. We established a trust that includes our business and personal assets. It designates who does what and who gets what for generations to come.

My financial legacy includes the following: The Financial Cures System, The Financial Cures Book Series, Master Classes, Mini Classes, trademarks, copyrights, a global streaming TV Show, music, poetry, videos, other businesses, and assets.

Enjoy life and do what you want to do when you want to do it. Life is too short to waste time complaining about what's wrong. Be grateful for what's right in your life.

Cure Your Financial Ills

Facebook.com/DrWendyLabat   Instagram.com/dr.wendy.labat
LinkedIn.com/DrWendyLabat

What's your free offer for cancer patients? *

Text "guide" to 770-796-4949 to get a complimentary guide "6 Ways to Stop Hemorrhaging Money"

Chapter 4

Discover Your Superpower Within

Coach M.J.Tolan

Coach M. J. Tolan

Mr. I'M Possible

Orlando, Florida, USA

Worldclastsi@gmail.com

> *Be bold in everything you do. When you do, the enemy will hear your confidence coming from miles away and run for cover.*
>
> *~Coach MJ*

Pure Survival Mode

Actually, my life before cancer was a rollercoaster. One of my business interest investments had totally melted down.

At the same time, my children who were living in Beirut with their mother were thinking about attending a university in the USA.

You won't believe this next bit, but you can check it on Google. Within a few months in this timeline, all of the banks in Lebanon, where my wife was from and had lived in our family home for over 25 years, collapsed.

All our life savings we had socked away were in those banks. They had been paying handsome interest rates for years, double anywhere else in the region. The currency took an immediate nosedive to devalue, and assets such as houses and lands could not be sold because no one had money to buy them. I came to the US thinking I could save the day. Why not? I could be hired as a trainer or speaker.

I had not worked for anyone or even worked in the US for over 35 years. Most people who looked at my new resume could not even pronounce some of the countries I had lived and worked in.

After getting some makeshift part-time job, thinking that things would get better, maybe just the banks would release the money. I was even hoping I would get a better job. Then, bang, Covid happened!

Now no one was hiring speakers or trainers, no audiences, and no choices, no hope.

It was off to YouTube university to learn how to do a zoom call. I started a Podcast. Ironically, I set out to interview people who had overcome incredible adversity. I named it 'The Real Mission: I'M Possible Show'. I was mentally living in Hope Island, (LA LA Land) meaning hoping that things would get better, I would get a better job, the banks would fix themselves, and the tooth fairy would leave diamonds under my pillow.

Kept My Poker Face
As I had lived overseas, I did not receive the memo that people should have a colonoscopy after the age of 45. One day in the summer of 2021 I experienced dampness in my pants and went to the men's room to check and found some blood. Something clicked inside me to jump to a clinic instantly and check it while a part of me thought I might be overreacting.

I was immediately encouraged at the clinic to have the exam to check the colon. As soon as I woke up, I heard a doctor ask, " Would you like the good news or the bad news first?"

Just like that! I said, ``of course, give me the bad news" (because I am a warrior and nothing could ever phase me).

Discover Your Superpower Within

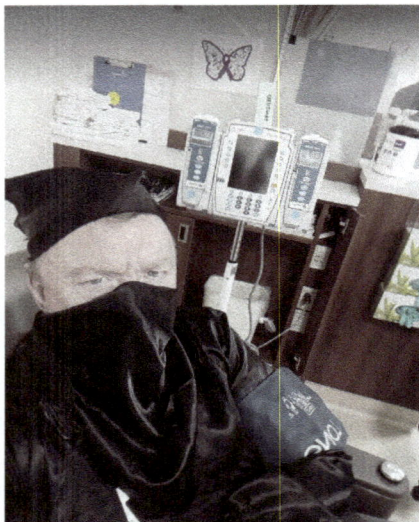

So he said, " You have cancer " which shocked me totally.
I felt as if I had been kicked in the gut.

And then, with a poker face, I asked, "So what is the good news?

He replied… "Well, Now we know!"

It was confirmed to be Stage 3C Rectal/Colon Cancer.

Find Your Faith
I went through "the why me question" especially after all of the punches I had received in my investments, the banks, the meltdown of the country of Lebanon, not finding it easy to get a high-level job, then Covid, and now this … Now mortality!?

My final curtain?
What the heck is going on !!!
I have been a student of affirmations long before, and I coached in my workshops on the power of affirmations also.

Did I believe them? Of course, it is easy to doubt when you feel you are drowning.

I looked for my faith. I grabbed hold of the smallest, tiniest of twigs.

I prayed. I prayed some more. I prayed again. I meditated and prayed. I prayed when I opened my eyes and before I closed them every night. I searched and searched and searched through prayer to find my faith.

The 'Why Me?" transformed into "Why Not Me?" and then into "Who Better than Me?"

Discover Your Superpower Within

Refuse to Surrender

There was a moment when I realized I was going to fight my way out and use everything I had ever learned about the mind and the power of prayer and healing. I would be tested, but I would not be broken. I had my own inspirational battle cry.

"I'M Possible". I became a cancer warrior, like a fireman, who is trained to be on alert and to risk his life to save others. Now it was my turn.

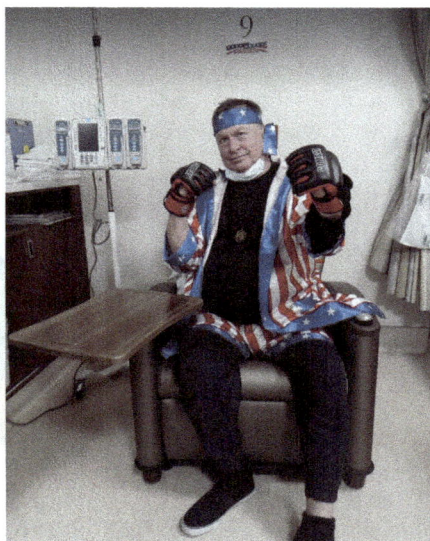

I knew I had to find the courage deep inside me to fight this un-invited invader. I went into warrior mode. I refused to attend support groups because I recognized: "My Journey is Different, M.J.I.D."

MY JOURNEY IS DIFFERENT

So throughout my entire journey of Chemo, I had pre-planned that I was going to be the one attacking cancer with humor and courage. I confess that at times FEAR did visit me as well as his best friend DOUBT.

They are a silly bunch. They are LIARS and THIEVES. They lie about the positive possibilities and rob you of your power to fight them off… But I had found FAITH, and I was not playing by the game's rules. I wore a new costume every week to march into the hospital. I passed by all the security, receptionists, clinical nurses, and doctors to receive my gift of Chemo.

I wore a different warrior costume every week. One week I was a Samurai Warrior, the next week I was a Gladiator, and another week I was a Knight of the Templars. It continued week after week until the staff could not wait to see what I would be wearing next!

Discover Your Superpower Within

Often some of the patients would see me and give me back a little wink, just enough as if to say " Keep it up for all of us" and I did!
I knew I was on my own crusade against FEAR, against HELPLESSNESS, and against ADVICE that everyone had when their Aunt Bertha, rest her soul, went through it.

Forget it! No way, Jose! I hired Mindset Coach Dr. Sofie Nubani.
This was war! I prepared my costumes as battle armor and wore them with sincere defiance.
The word is Defiance!
I refused to be a helpless cancer patient.

Gratitude has Power
We all talk about it, and it is a bit cliche because you know whenever you read a slogan on a coffee mug or a t-shirt … well, you get it.' However, when intentionally practicing the use of guided meditation, when purposefully reciting what we really have to be grateful for, and when we are able to make a list, that list we are most grateful to have… we can see our real wealth.

One thing about Covid and the Damndemic taught us all was that the things we most valued yesterday really do not matter as much as we thought.

Our Values Are Everything! My Great Mom was my Teacher!

Lessons I Learned
We must be the DJ of our Life; if we are not, someone else will play the music that we could never manage to dance to …

FEAR needs food.
Starve it to Death
by not buying any
of the stories that
his cousin, Mr.
DOUBT, has to sell.

Discover Your Superpower Within

Cancer is a COWARD; it is terrified of Bravery and Frightened of a good sense of humor. Buy a joke book if you have to but get laughing quickly as you can.

Stay away from people who will try to give you any advice about what their Aunt Bertha went through …Run and close your ears.

Find your power in being alone; your inner stillness to meditate, pray, affirm, and breathe.

Never Back Down
It is evident that I have been given a new chance to give back, tell this story, and inspire anyone who is fearful of the journey.

I felt an almost bursting impulse to get as much of

my knowledge and input out to the world during treatments. Now I have my own story and will be elaborating on this trip a bit more in a new book.Oh, it does feel different telling someone that I had cancer when it is said in the past tense. It feels awesome. I felt it was imperative to celebrate the victory by ringing both bells, Chemo and Radiation.

At each ceremony I had requested Rocky music and was dressed in character, wearing boxing gloves with full Rocky trunks and cape and shouting ADRIAN on my way to ring that bell.

But I did it.

I rang it LOUDLY. I had practiced ringing it before, every day.

Discover Your Superpower Within

Courage, I often say, is when your knees are shakin', but you take a step forward anyway.

Yeah, so you have a choice. Get eaten by hiding from the fear monster or go courageously and fight the unknown dragon.

Go Kill the Dragon!

Steps For Your Journey
1. Decide this is your journey; you define it; and you control your inner journey.
2. Understand that fear, self-doubt, self-pity, and helplessness are all going to show up, but they are not welcome.
3. Become a fan of seeing the funny side of all of this. I actually as part of my own self-healing therapy challenged myself to an open mic night at a comedy club just to share the "good news and bad news story". It was a riot!
4. Stay Grateful. Remain Faithful.

Our attitude is everything. It will be the best GPS we can ever use, but it must have the power of faith tuning in on gratitude radio. This has real healing power; trust in this, believe this and do this.

If not you, who?
Practicing self-love? That is easy. If not sending love to you, then who else?

I remember when I heard Brian Tracy say, "If it's to be, it's up to me."

This means that no one is coming to the rescue. In the game of life, you got tagged; now you are it. You cannot hide from that and wish it away, but there is no superhero coming to save the day...
Unless... You allow 'you' to become your very own superhero.

You are the only one who can save you, and it all depends on your DJ, your attitude of gratitude, your positive mindset, and your sense of humor, and this is who you need to be right now!

In my experience, I treated myself with love and care every time I put on my costume.

Discover Your Superpower Within

In my experience, when I was faced with going to radiation every day, I changed the name of that clinic to the Spa.

I was visiting the spa… Self-Love.

I even bought the fluffy spa slippers.
Do you know a 5-star hotel spa and the fluffy robe outfits?
Yep, I had those also. While other patients were going to receive radiation treatment, I refused to buy that narrative.

Spa Day, Ladies, here I am. :)

Remember other People! They feel Awkward!
They don't have any experience to know how to support you except:
They worry and look nervous.
They are Not sure what to say.
They will repeat something they heard on Dr. Oz or Oprah.
They will bless you.

Be the pillar of power and strength that gives them all reassurance that you got this and follow my 2 Keys… Laughter and Defiance. Allow them to feel they can also joke about this whole scenario and give them ammunition to laugh it off with you …

Remaining Defiant means remembering you did not sign a lease to rent out a part of your body to strangers who were uninvited to your birthday and Christmas party so…never accept tenancy, call Orkin, and get them critters OUT!

Support Was Not My Thing
No Comment as I did not use support groups any at all, ever. This was not my scene or strategy, but it might be good for some. Every trip is different. Ask any Uber driver. I did have my phenomenal 7 Tolan Brothers, best friends in the world, so blessed. We are the Great 8!

Start From Here
Remember monopoly---the board game? You roll the dice, and then you get a card that says… Go Directly to Jail, Do not Pass Go, Do Not Collect 200.00 Dollars …

Discover Your Superpower Within

Life is a game in many ways, especially if you want to win the mind set game.

Are you a victim or are you the victor?

I did not work during all of this and missed it. So now as I return out of hibernation and begin to look into reconnecting my professional life back into the game, I am starting all over in many ways, but wait... do you know anyone who did not make it out of the pandemic?

Start Over with Credentials ... You Won!

I look forward to bringing my battle scars with me wherever I go.

However, this journey was mine, and I am not defined by this as a tragedy that happened to me, oh poor me. Really? Surely Not!

I went through it, ok. I survived and thrived, Thank the Lord...But I look for the next new chapter of my life that I have been given...

*New Possibilities because I'M Possible.

❝

Remember the first three letters of
cancer are: C a n !
Can Do! "

Coach McJ

"Folks, don't take any of this too seriously, this game of life. lit has already been proven that no one is getting out alive anyway, but...
while you are here, have as much fun as you can and laugh loud and often. I promise you it scares those critters away :)
*Hire me to speak with your organization or club.

Discover Your Superpower Within

Chapter 5

Ella Solo Amor

(She Was Pure Love)

Raquel G. Ramirez

Raquel G. Ramirez
Mom
Laredo, Texas Webb County
Carlosrenermz@gmail.com or rita.rmz15@gmail.com

Ella Solo Amor
(She Was Pure Love)

In Memory of Raquel G. Ramirez known as …
Mom
Mane (grandmother's nickname)
'Wifa'/Honey
Coyotita (nickname from her parents)

Coauthors

Husband: Carlos Rene Ramirez
Children: Carlos Rene Ramirez Jr, +Raguel Ramirez, Raquel Ramirez Torres, Rita Ramirez, Carlos Roberto Ramirez, Rebecca Ramirez Vera, Carlos Ricardo Ramirez, Carlos Rodolfo Ramirez
Grandchildren: Desiree Alina Torres, Sophia Alana Torres, Nathan Allen Torres, Alicia Alayla Torres, Amelia Rocio Torres, Emma Leah Lopez & Baby Mateo Lorenzo Vera

> **The old saying, "Laughter is the best medicine" isn't a metaphor. It's a precious human truth.**

Ella Solo Amor
(She Was Pure Love)

Devoted Mom and Community Member

She worked for the Laredo Independent School District for 36 years, starting as a Librarian, moving on as a Parent Liaison, and finishing off as a Guitar/Choir Teacher. She also helped provide music for the parent courses led by her husband Carlos Rene Ramirez. She was a devoted member of the community and was a firm believer in the unity of family to which the City of Laredo has honored both Carlos Rene and Raquel by renaming the Santo Niño WIC Clinic to "Carlos Rene & Raquel G. Ramirez WIC Clinic & Health Center" this past May 24, 2022.

Raquel was very brave and courageous after battling all that she went through. She underwent seven births, one miscarriage, eight chemo sessions, thirty-three radiation sessions, and nineteen surgeries. She suffered through many changes— physical and mental. Even through the loss of her parents and the illness she encountered,she

never lost her faith. She took everything head-on and faced every adversity with dignity and grace. Her smile, love, and presence are great and truly missed each day by those who knew her best.

The Ramirez tribe is here to remind you of the importance of family and support and to keep going no matter where the road leads you. You have what it takes to overcome any obstacles life may throw at you.

Family First

Rita Ramirez, Raquel's fourth daughter out of eight and second oldest daughter, remembers her mom this way:

Life before cancer is so hard to truly remember. What I can remember is that it was much less stressful, and I didn't worry whether or not my mom was going to die. I was 14 years old when she first got diagnosed, and my parents were very involved with our extracurricular activities and our sporting events. After the diagnosis, their presence at every game or event became that much sweeter and more appreciated.

Ella Solo Amor
(She Was Pure Love)

The effect it had on me has stayed with me still to this day. I had always been a "worrisome" person, but when my Mom got diagnosed with cancer, that was the first time I ever experienced anxiety. I had never really known what that felt like until I was feeling it every day since her diagnosis. I remember we were not supposed to speak of it until we had all the full details, and it was so hard to keep it together. I remember the day I finally told my closest friends, my inner circle, what was truly going on with me, and for once I felt a little weight lifted. My parents are loved and well-known by my friends. They would call them Mom and Dad at one point so when I finally shared the news, they had the same reaction. We were standing outside in the school courtyard, huddled up and crying. I was taken to the counselor's office where I spent most of my days. I couldn't think straight, I couldn't focus, and I couldn't stop crying. It got to the point where I had to make the hard decision to leave sports. Sadly, I tried to see if I could stay in sports, but I would have had to miss sometimes because of my mom's illness, and I was told I had to be present 100% of the time or not at all. I chose NOT AT ALL on the spot. It was a quick and easy decision because I wasn't going to put anything above my mom or family. It still saddens me, but I do not regret it.

Now at 30 years old, I still have anxiety today even though it has been 3 years and 8 months without her. I still feel as if I'm a lost little girl looking and yearning for her mom. So to any educators or coaches reading this, my suggestion is to allow student-athletes to continue with their sports and be able to provide that safe space and outlet for them in order to help them release stress and anxiety from their reality. Don't make them choose, but be there to provide them a safe haven and comfort away from home which will fill their hearts with joy and relief even if it is for a moment.

68

Ella Solo Amor
(She Was Pure Love)

Heaven Calling

My mom, Raquel G. Ramirez, was diagnosed for the first time on February 25, 2008, with stage 2 breast cancer. The way she found out was through her annual medical exam which showed that the breast cancer was caused by a clogged milk duct. She fought hard and remained in remission for a few years, and then around her 10th year in remission, in December 2017, she was diagnosed for the second time with metastatic breast cancer stage 4. The cancer had spread to her pelvis which ultimately caused her hip to fracture. For months on end, she couldn't walk or stand. She was wheelchair-bound for a while, and that really dimmed her light. She relied on us to help her get around, and I saw how hard that was for her. Luckily, she was able to have a full hip replacement, and she was able to walk and dance again which made her and us happy. After that, she began to decline, and we wanted to try to get a second opinion which led us to try to get her to MD Anderson. Unfortunately, they were not able to help her. I remember the facetime family meeting we had when we were told the news, and I felt as if my whole world shattered once again. We tried our best to keep her comfortable, make her laugh, distract her, and pray for and with her, but I could see the anxiety and turmoil in her eyes. I remember begging God for a miracle, saying that if anyone deserved one, it would be her. Lamentably, cancer overcame her body, and she passed away on March 28, 2019, at 4:30 a.m. surrounded by her family who had one hand on her, singing to her so that she would be able to go in peace.

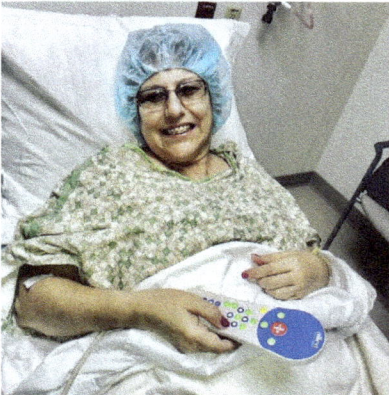

Although we know that our time will end one day, the best thing to do is live in our moment and appreciate life and the people around us. It is scary when you are actually given a time frame because we count every second. Remember to stop, breathe, and make sure you tell your loved ones how much you love them. Don't hold back to discover a way to express yourself and live life to the fullest.

Continuous Healing

My name is Rebecca Ramirez Vera, also known as Becky. I am the daughter of Raquel G. Ramirez. I am the sixth child out of her eight children, and I am also the youngest daughter out of three. Fun fact, I am also known as the "tiebreaker" as my parents called me since there were already two girls and two boys.

Ella Solo Amor
(She Was Pure Love)

My healing journey has been challenging, and I think that it will always be. It's a constant battle I fight every day. I see it everywhere and am reminded of it almost daily. We see the fight in many strong individuals, and you can see how much it has affected their lives. I was so young when my mom was first diagnosed. I was only ten years old. I didn't understand what cancer meant at the time. My younger siblings and I struggled to try to understand what happens when a person is diagnosed with cancer and how much it affects not only the individual but the support system she has. Some days I'm okay to breathe again and stand tall; other days I'm reliving the last moments in my head, and I'm broken down all over again. The healing never ends. We just learn to live with it and adjust our lives to the change it has brought. Sometimes it's sad that nowadays there are movies created where the mom is battling cancer, specifically breast cancer. It makes me feel so many emotions, and I'm reminded of what cancer took from me. I try every day to take it one day at a time. I try to give myself time to let me feel my emotions and to remind myself it's okay if I'm not strong today. I can be strong tomorrow. I let myself grieve, feel, express, explode, and just not feel the pressure of having to be okay all the time. It would drive me crazy if I allowed myself to heal the way others would want me to heal and how they would want me to heal. I remind myself that my healing journey is only mine to experience, and it will only go at the pace that it needs to go. Healing involves all five stages of grief, but the healing doesn't end when you've crossed through each stage.

The healing journey continues, and it is a journey in which everyone's experience is unique. It should never be rushed, cut short, or disregarded. The healing journey allows you to persevere and overcome whatever life throws at you. It helps you transition into new phases of life, sometimes for the better or sometimes for the worst. Not every healing journey will be a walk in the park, but it will help you grow, learn, and accept. For those of you healing, there is no right or wrong way to process the heartaches you endured

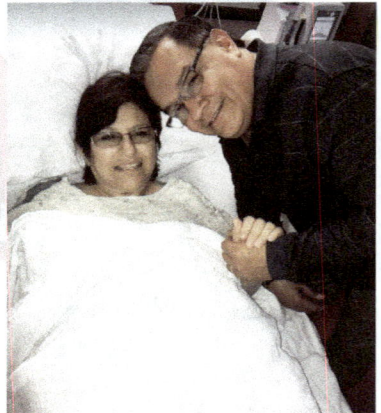

The important thing is to allow yourself to grieve but also to move forward. Just because you move forward doesn't mean you forget–that just means you are strong enough to continue living.

Ella Solo Amor
(She Was Pure Love)

From Carlos Roberto Ramirez: +JMJ

My mom and I have always been close, even to this day. Since the moment of my difficult birth, my dad has always said, "

"Your pregnancy, birth, and fight for survival brought your mom to the complete Circle of Motherhood." I saved her life, but the feeling was mutual as she gave me the will to live. That bonded us so closely for life.The day God called my mom to Himself was by far the most challenging day I've had to endure, but the comfort in all this was that I was able to have one last beautiful conversation with my mom before she passed. I was afraid, and I didn't know what was going to happen. I went to her bedside somewhat sobbing, but quietly as I didn't wish to wake her. She heard me and asked me what was wrong. I explained my unknown fear to her. She quickly got up and told me, "Be not afraid. Am I not here? I'm with you, and I love you! How many times in the Scripture does it say to 'Be not afraid'? 365 times, one for every day. So be not afraid. I am here, and I love you." Her last words were 'Be not afraid, resonate in my heart daily. Coping with her loss has been difficult, but there is a sense of peace in knowing and believing in my heart that my mom is a saint in heaven. Every time I get to partake in the Holy Sacrifice of the mass, I know she is by my side praying with me. That has brought so much comfort. My ultimate hope is that as each day passes, I am one day closer to seeing her again in heaven with all its glory to be united with my earthly and heavenly mother.

Find comfort in "be not afraid". Discover hope of one-day reuniting with your loved ones. Remember they are always with you so live life and honor their legacy.

Trusting God's Plan

My name is Rebecca Ramirez Vera, also known as Becky, the youngest daughter.

What I took from this journey is that tomorrow is never promised. It changed the way I view life now. The strength I saw within my mom was greater than I could ever imagine. It was amazing and crazy, and I was awestruck by how strong she was through her fight. The love she spread and still continued to do so even when she was feeling emotional, mental, and physical exhaustion brought so much light, love, peace, happiness, strength, courage, life, faith, hope, humility, perseverance, and support. She made it a mission to stand tall and be strong. She made it known that her faith would not falter, and her love for God will always be greater.

Ella Solo Amor
(She Was Pure Love)

She trusted God's plan. She prayed and used her life to love God through it all. She kept her faith strong and always praised Him. She was a force of nature for other individuals battling the same cancer and was their support. I learned so much from my mom that I'm so blessed, honored, grateful, and thankful that I'm her daughter. She always shared with me "Let go and let God". I learned more about my faith through her battle with cancer. Without my faith in God and my love for Him, I wouldn't have been able to overcome losing my mom to cancer. As of today, I still feel every emotion you can think of, but I have God ready to catch me every time I fall. My mom was a superhero. She was my guiding light. She always reminded me, "You are your mother's daughter. You're strong and beautiful, and you can do anything your heart desires. Let go and let God. Fall in love with Jesus." She was a woman of God. She loved my dad and her kids unconditionally. She always reminded us how loved we were.

There's so much that I have learned from her all 21 years of my life. My mother's love was/is powerful. She was/is loved by so many people. I'm so blessed by the many lives she's impacted and made a difference in.

St. Augustine said in Spanish, "**Ama y haz lo que quieras**. Si callas, callarás con amor; si gritas, gritarás con amor; si corriges, corregirás con amor; si perdonas, perdonarás con amor which means Love and do what you want. If you shut up, you will shut up with love; if you scream, you will scream with love; if you correct, you will correct with love; if you forgive, you will forgive with love. Remember to let faith be bigger than your fears.

From Carlos Roberto Ramirez:+JMJ
The most profound lesson I learned is that life is so fragile, and we are all going to suffer in this life. But that reality brought many graces, especially for mom; after all, she faithfully and courageously endured because St. Ignatius of Loyola once said, "If God sends you many sufferings, it is a sign that He has great plans for you and certainly wants to make you a saint." There is no doubt that my mom is a saint

Ella Solo Amor
(She Was Pure Love)

in heaven. Looking back, I can see a saint in the making, perhaps not through rigorous piety although she had a deep love for God and held fast to prayer in all her trials and joys through redemptive suffering.

She once used a line from St. Pope John Paul II about making sure she wasn't wasting her suffering. It was always geared towards redemptive suffering which she lovingly offered. Even though we saw Mom suffer throughout the years with cancer, she remained forever joyful even in the midst of that suffering. Nothing would phase her. No surgery, no treatment, and no difficulty would ever remove her sincere joy. Of course, this all affected her humanity in depriving her of the comfort of peace and healing, yet she lovingly embraced her cross and fought courageously to the end even to her last breath as we cheered her on to heaven where I believe she dwells. I learned that redemptive suffering is a gift from God, and for one who lives it, like my mom so lovingly did, heaven awaits.

We don't know why God calls us to suffer sometimes, but we must trust his plan, find joy in all aspects regardless of the pain, and remember that heaven awaits.

From: Carlos Ricardo Ramirez, seventh child out of eight.
There was this one time I was driving late at night heading towards Houston, Texas, where I lived at the time. It was dark, and I saw a light far in the distance. I was fixated on it when all of a sudden, a song came on the radio called, "On Eagle's Wings". That song would play on Saturdays when Mom would clean early mornings. As I drove closer, that light in the distance took the form of a hand in the shape of "I Love You" in American Sign Language. My mom was very well known for that; no matter what, she always made that sign for us. Whether we were leaving, finishing a sports game, or even simply recording her, she always made that sign. Seeing that sign made me feel happy and assured me that it was her way of saying she was still there for me.

Our loved ones might have passed on but always look for signs that they are among us and letting us know that they haven't left our side. You might want to choose a symbol or phrase that you can use to pass on to your family and friends which will live on even after you are gone.

Ella Solo Amor
(She Was Pure Love)

From Raquel Ramirez Torres, third child out of eight and the oldest daughter.

Every day I live is a day to honor Mom. There was something so attractive in my mom. It was her positive energy. She could light up a room, and she had a smile and laugh that could change your day. It didn't matter what setting we were in, the pureness in her heart was seen by those she helped. In my transition from an educator to a registered nurse, I honor her by providing patients with a caring and positive attitude and by sharing a simple smile. Even a smile can be seen through the mask because of the tenderness and caring service being provided. I listen with my heart, and many times it has been enough to give them hope. Although it's not easy, taking on that attitude Mom had and aiming to do something that will help others, has molded me into the person I am today.

From Carlos Rodolfo Ramirez, youngest child

Throughout the tough journey of cancer, there are four steps to playing the game of life, and those steps are to Live, Laugh, Love, and have fun. Live the only way you know how because at the end of the day, you know who you are, and there is only one life so just live it. Laugh! As they say, laughter is the best medicine. When you laugh even if it is for a brief moment, everything will go away, and you will be left with just a feeling of happiness. Love is a powerful force that is unmatched. It is something everyone needs if he/she is going to win the game of life. To be surrounded by loved ones in your most challenging stage, there is a sense of peace in knowing you are loved. So love as much as you can because life is precious, and once you are no longer here, it leaves a crater in your heart where the love was filled. When in doubt—LOVE! The final step to winning in this game we call life is having FUN. Life is too short to

Be feeling trapped.

Find something you really enjoy and expand on that. See how far it takes you. Expand your horizons and get out of your comfort zone to the best of your ability

and enjoy it. Life is about trying new things and gaining new experiences. So when all else fails, just have fun.

Ella Solo Amor
(She Was Pure Love)

As long as you feel happy and are enjoying yourself, you have already won no matter the outcome. I know my mom Raquel G. Ramirez won at life. She Lived, Laughed, and Loved, and had Fun. No matter what the outcome was she knew in her heart she had lived life to the fullest every single day, and it was so inspiring to see her glowing even on days when she did not feel 100%. If you follow these rules in life just one day at a time, you will win in life.

From Rita Ramirez, third child out of eight and second oldest daughter.
My mom was in her last semester at Texas A&M International University studying for her bachelor's degree in music when she first got diagnosed with breast cancer. She was halfway through completing her studies when what felt like a huge and unexpected weight not just for her but for all of us became a full halt We were left completely stunned by the news and didn't know what was to be expected. After we had ridden on what was a very heavy emotional roller coaster and medical plans had been set in place, my mother had to make the decision of whether she would continue and finish or again stop and attend to her health and needs. One thing about my mom's educational background was it took her twenty-six years to finish that degree. Why do you ask? Well, she has always been a big believer in the family over everything. Having eight children while trying to finish school was hard enough so she always chose family, hence why it took her this long. By this time, her youngest was five, and her three oldest ones were teenagers who would always help as much as we could. With that, the decision was made to go forth and finally finish school and once and for all graduate with her bachelor's degree in music. We all reassured her and told her we would be there every single step of the way. That was motivating for her and very much needed for all of us. Before my mother was diagnosed, she said she would graduate in pink because she wanted to have one last child, a girl, but when the time came, she said, "I am graduating in pink but not for a baby girl but in pink to honor breast cancer" because that is the color of the ribbon itself. I remember the extensive work she put in to be able to attend classes and finish homework along with the eight chemo sessions she needed to undergo. After her second chemo session, she began to lose all her hair, and she decided to have her oldest son, Carlos Renee, Jr., shave it all off.

Instead of crying, she decided to make jokes and laugh about her hair loss because, for her, laughter truly was the best medicine. She was worried for a bit because she had a very important final coming up.

Ella Solo Amor
(She Was Pure Love)

Being a music major meant that as part of a final, you needed to partake in a necessary recital, in my mother's case, a voice recital in front of all her instructors and judges. Usually, students would request a closed recital because of how intense it was. but we decided to turn it into something positive and supportive for my mom. My dad had the amazing idea of having family, friends, and people who wanted to support my mom attend the recital, but everyone was to wear pink. and we all wore little pink breast cancer ribbons. The day finally came on April 19, 2008. The auditorium was filled; every seat was taken with what looked like a pink ocean. Everyone showed up, dressed accordingly, and even had supportive messages and flowers for her. It was an unbelievable sight to see the overwhelming love and support my mom had that evening. What made it even more special was that it was my late grandmother's birthday who was her mother. She had suffered a horrible accident that left her disabled and suffered from Alzheimer's, so having her present meant the world to my mom, and at the end of it, she got to gift my grandmother flowers and even sing her a serenade the way she had sung since my mom was fifteen years old. The love and support my mom had not only that day but every day was and always will be appreciated by the Ramirez Tribe.

From, Rita Ramirez.
My mom always called me her cheerleader because I was always making her cards for everything. I would write her little notes saying how proud of her I was, how much I believed in her, and how much I loved her. When she had surgery, I would make big colorful signs and have my family sign and leave loving and motivating messages. If she were to be away from home for a few days, we would decorate with homemade banners to welcome her home as well. I tried everything to keep her motivated, inspired, and loved during the cancer years.

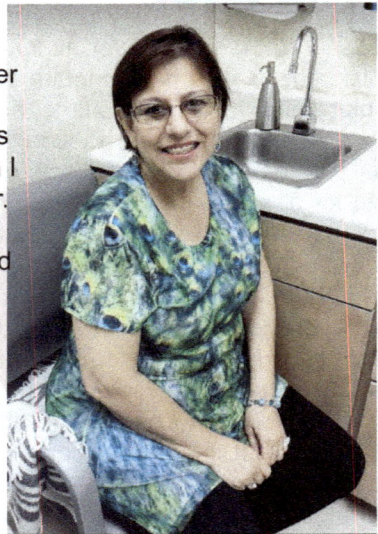

One of the projects I made for her was a container filled with colorful index cards and handwritten messages from family and friends who took the time to leave a beautiful message for her to read on days that were the hardest. My advice would be to love your family member and friends dealing with cancer and make them something special that comes from you; keep them in your prayers.

Ella Solo Amor
(She Was Pure Love)

Make sure they are not alone, that they don't feel like a burden, and that no matter what, you will always be there to walk with them every step of the way.

Outside Support

My mom received help from an organization called Pink To Do which helped my family during the hardships especially when it came down to necessities and other things needed. This helped my family a lot because there were times when my family was in much need, and Mrs. Narvaez helped us out by providing what was needed at the time, for example, groceries and other necessities. My mom lost a lot of days of work because of the illness, therefore, making her payroll smaller and smaller. This is why we are forever grateful for all that Pink To Do has done for us. There is another organization that was just created called Stronger Together which helps those affected by breast cancer.

From Carlos Rene Ramirez Jr.

The support systems I'd recommend for families going through breast cancer are local foundations and local nonprofits that focus on mental and emotional support, cover medical bills, and assist in providing day-to-day necessities like groceries. My mother, Raquel G. Ramirez, and my family were blessed to receive such help from the organization Pink To Do with Mrs. Martha Narvaez. They were instrumental in alleviating some of the financial strains of paying for doctor visits and surgeries. Through Pink To Do's compassion and assistance, my family was able to focus on my mother's recovery and not get overwhelmed with bills or stressed from not having enough food for the week.

From Raquel Ramirez Torres.

The legacy left behind is in her music. She left us with original songs that have helped us get through tough times but also understand our own feelings through song. Many people will recall the beautiful voice she shared with the world.

Ella Solo Amor
(She Was Pure Love)

> **"** —————
>
> *Stuart Scott said in his 2014 Espy Award Speech, "When you die, it does not mean that you lose to cancer; you beat cancer by how you live, why you live, and in the manner in which you live."*

Words of encouragement

From Raquel Ramirez Torres.

Cancer can be beaten! It is not the end. Stay positive; take it one day at a time. Every day you live is a day you beat cancer. Family and friends, if you have loved ones who are going through this, be their shoulder so they can lean on you; be patient, be loving, and share a smile or happy thoughts daily. Remind the person that he or she is loved.

FB: Carlos Rene Ramirez and also Carlos Rene Ramirez Sr.

Chapter 6

Hope

Jeff Cade

Jeff Cade

Healthy Lifestyle Specialist

CHICAGO. IL USA

jcade1911@gmail.com

Hope

> ❝———
>
> *CANCER- There's CAN in the Word..Yes you CAN!*
> *You CAN Beat This!*

My Name is Jeff Cade. My Team and I empower and partner with people to transform unhealthy choices into an active vibrant Lifestyle by joining our 360HealthandWellnessnetwork.com. You'll experience and engage in a 7-week moduled-based program focusing on the Mindset, Diet, and exercise to allow a transformative process.

PUSH- Persist Until Something Happens!
WIN- What's Important NOW?

I'm a Healthy Lifestyle Specialist, award-winning Author, and Coach. I've been in the Hospitality Industry and Wellness space for over 15 years and Co-Owned a Healthy restaurant concept. I have been featured on multiple podcasts and radio broadcasts sharing my message on living a Healthier powered lifestyle.

Cancer Claimed My Parents' Lives
Before Cancer, we took Family vacations when allowed, and they enjoyed each other's company. It was everyday " normal" activities from work, school, and possible meetings for them, and play time for me during my

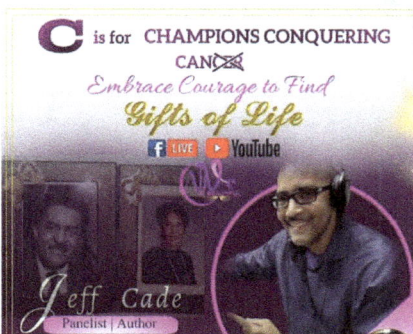

youth. Both parents served in different capacities within their communities.
My Mother was diagnosed in 1987, and I was in my 2nd year away in college and afraid, numb, and uncertain of her Longevity. Thankfully God blessed and graced her 10 more years before succumbing to breast cancer in 1997.

Hope

My father received his diagnosis of pancreatic cancer during that time frame, but at Stage 3 and passed in 1991.

He was my Hero, and she was my SheRo! I was lost and my heart sank. I didn't want to finish college but finished the task in 1992. During his life, my father referenced that time waits for no one; enjoy Life every day. They both passed in their middle 60s. To this day I miss and value their parental love, touch, and guidance!

Both of my parents were diagnosed with cancer during my Youth. Unfortunately, they passed 6 years apart. My father died from Pancreatic and my mother from Breast Cancer.

My mother was diagnosed in 1987 with Breast Cancer, and she underwent general treatment with radiation and chemotherapy. She went through a double mastectomy, and God gave her 10 more years. During that time frame, she engaged in holistic support via acupuncture and drank Chinese herbal black tea. She passed in 1997.

Keep the Faith

Believe in a Power higher than yourself, and Keep the Faith. The Battle is not yours; it's the Lord's! Refer to the power of I AM Affirmations with Intention and Purpose. I enjoy using them to motivate and center myself for self-care.

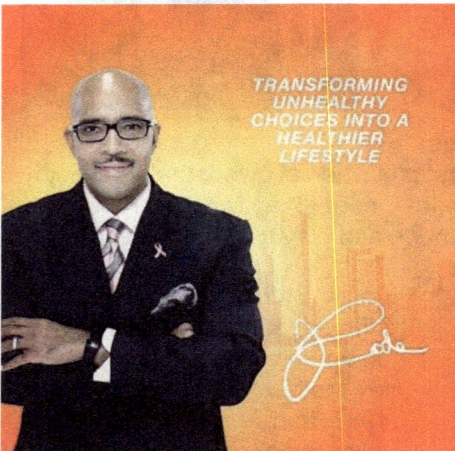

Here are some examples for you:

- I AM Amazing & Able.
- I AM Blessed & Beautiful
- I AM a Champion I AM Dedicated & Delivered
- I AM Exceedingly prosperous
- I AM Fearless & Faithful
- I AM Grateful I AM Healthy!

Whatever we think about we bring about. It starts and ends with our mind. Speak with a powerful tongue as our Universe is always listening. You can customize a variety of words for your personal experience and enjoyment.

Hope

Healing Journey

It was a tough road: mentally, emotionally and Spiritually. Navigating Life was very challenging. One moment your parents are with you, until they're NOT and you can't wrap your head around it while being an emotional wreck. I believe that God will never leave nor forsake you. Also that HE won't put you through something you can't handle. Through our testimonies, we all must go through TESTS. I leaned on him as I know he's my Rock and Salvation. I just couldn't understand my parents physical absence into spiritual essence. I also know that our bodies/temples are temporary on this Earth, and our spirits will reconnect with our Divine Heavenly Creator when it's time.

By bringing my thoughts and what was in my heart, I penned the book: "Battleground Cancer". It was therapeutic and empowering and impacted lives.

Speak and share content to bring awareness to your mindset, diet, and exercise routines. Serve and do more!

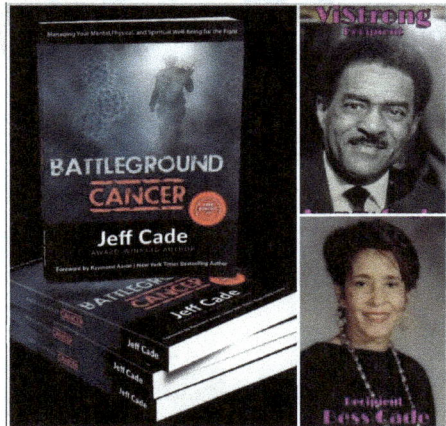

BATTLEGROUND
CANCER
Jeff Cade

4 Steps Cancer Patients can use to Play the Game of Life During Difficult Moments

1. Be Patient with yourself. The transformation process is yours to embrace.
2. Pray. Praying is Powerful and essential!
3. Let go. Let God. Your Time is not HIS; neither is your Thinking. He's the Author of your Life, so stop trying to steal the pen.
4. Be open-minded to Holistic alternative support. Do your Research and embrace other medical methods for Longevity purposes.

Why is it important to practice self-love?

Journal: Have an Attitude of Gratitude. God loves you unconditionally, so keep him first. Appreciate the small things and be in the Moment.

It was tough when my parents passed, and family members were shocked, of course. However, communication was key.

My Support System
My support system was my Family. During those dark periods, I was unaware of support groups, etc. Most of my family/friends had both parents or one in the household. I did what I thought was good for me and leaned on my family's shoulders and prayed for strength and protection.

I recommend the American Cancer Society and other organizations that focus on recovery and healing.

Leaving a Legacy
Besides using my book as a platform to share content, my Team and I created 360HealthandWellnessnetwork.com so people can be part of the Change and accelerate their Health goals to live a vibrant powered Lifestyle!

I'm Blessed by the BEST!

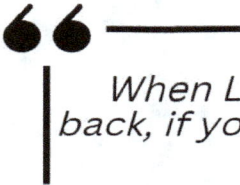

66 ——————

> *When Life knocks you down on your back, if you can look UP, you can Get UP!*

Jeff Cade

Words of Encouragement
Keep pushing and fighting for YOU! Cancer will not Win this battle for God is on your Side. He is your Rock!
Connect with me at Jeffcade360.com
to my social media outlets.

Free offer:

A Health Discovery Call at
www.360Healthandwellnessnetwork.com

Free Chapter of my book:
Battleground Cancer.

Chapter 7

Love Without Measure

Laura Fernandez Perez

Laura Fernández Pérez

Author | Supermom

Barcelona, Barcelona, Spain
lauraninefive59@gmail.com

Love Without Measure

My name is Laura. I help other people to remind them that they are capable of being everything they want by being true to themselves to live a fulfilling life full of confidence, harmony, and inner peace.

I am Laura, I was born in the Mediterranean, in Barcelona, Spain. I am the second of four sisters, having sisters is a gift. My little family is made up of my beloved daughter Sara and our beloved Elvis, a fun and loving poodle who is a four-legged angel. I have been living in L.A. for a while and there I met the man who would be my husband, we lived for a while in Mexico City where I really enjoyed resuming my professional career as a model. I returned to Barcelona after a few years and we finally parted ways.

I dedicated myself to interior decoration, among many other jobs over time. Currently, I still have not been able to return to work, although I am dedicating time to developing my future work, since I have trained as a life coach and NLP, it is my desire to be a ray of light, faith, and hope.

Stress, Struggle and Love

Throughout my life, I have always been dedicated to giving the best of myself. My greatest satisfaction has been and continues to be providing my daughter with everything she needs: values, respect, education, and emotional stability. I grew up in a dysfunctional family and that significantly marked my self-esteem and beliefs.

Love Without Measure

Being a single mother requires great commitment and dedication, although it has been the most wonderful experience of my life. Overall my life has been hard and I have had to have courage and courage, I know what it is to suffer sexist violence, live in fear, with stress maintained over time, in times of economic difficulties and survival situations where my working life was of great physical effort and also mentally exhausting. Undoubtedly, all this affects physical, emotional, and mental health, nothing is separate, everything is united.

Also, on the other hand, I was able to discover abilities and talents that boosted me by increasing my inner strength and recognizing the most creative parts within me. Always getting over myself no matter how exhausted I felt. I know that cancer I have overcome, thank God, was the product of stress and suffering.

Blessed, Loved, and Grateful.
One Tuesday, September 22, I was going to work, and the feeling of walking down the street after the confinement was strange and bleak. I always walk at a good pace, not to say running. I only needed to cross a traffic light to get to the bus stop, I made a maneuver to get ahead and I stepped on the sidewalk badly, falling to the ground. I felt a great pain in my right foot and my water bottle was thrown by the impulse. I got up and I thought that I had only sprained my foot, I continued on my way, and when I got to work I cleaned and healed the wound on my left knee. Soon after, I felt the pain in my foot increase until it was unbearable. I have always told myself as Rocky "no pain, no pain", although this time something told me to go to the doctor. I took a taxi and went to the hospital. Result: foot fracture. At that time I asked the doctor if I could look at my left leg, since the calf part was very inflamed, for at least two years. I had an ultrasound and from the way, the doctor looked at me, I knew something was not right. They put my foot in a cast and I had to come back urgently the next day for an MRI with contrast.

Love Without Measure

On October 27, the doctor informs me that I have a 9-centimeter myxoid sarcoma. At that moment, my head shoots up and my heart seems to stop for an instant that seems eternal. The first thing I thought of was my daughter Sara. Later, there were thousands of thoughts in my mind split in two, a voice told me "everything is fine" and another voice "you can die".

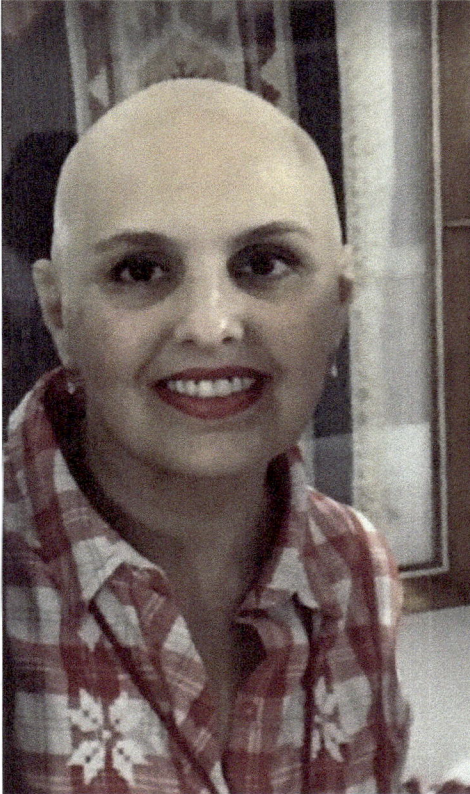

Seeds of Hope

In those moments of uncertainty, where everything seems to collapse, love is our great weapon, love for our loved ones to continue is our strength. We ourselves have all the ability to see with new eyes, allowing ourselves our beautiful vulnerable humanity and embracing it with our whole being. Trust, close your eyes, and visualize yourself full of life and perfect health. Appreciating the magnificent and loving work that our immune system, cells, and organs do.

Feeling the greatness of our being.Meditate. Laugh watching movies. Hug and hug yourself again and again, gently and warmly. Read. express yourself Listen to music, it has the gift of transporting you wherever you want. love yourself And feel a torrent of love within you.

Love Without Measure

God Sustains Me

From the first moment, and although I had many moments of fear when I found out that the tumor was inside me and all the time that it had accompanied me without knowing it. At no time did I feel rejection, on the contrary, I know it may seem very strange, but I accepted it out of love.

I never named it as most people do "the bug." I even hugged him. It was part of me and it was a blessing to fall, it had to be like that without a doubt. I thanked and am deeply grateful each new day for the immense and wonderful work that my body does, I apologize for having taken it to the maximum, demanding everything and more, and not having answered his calls.

In each chemotherapy and radiotherapy session, I helped my body through thoughts of gratitude, day by day, until the operation and feeling free and healed.

Thank you is my permanent attitude status.
Inside me, these words resonate with "my beloved and I are one" because God is my sustenance, strength, and inspiration. It is all my peace.

Love Without Measure

It All Starts Today

I have learned that putting myself off is not loving myself, that enduring to the limit does not help me, that stress sustained over time exhausts the spirit, that taking care of my body is an absolute priority, and that it deserves all the maximum care and love. It is our temple and he quietly asks us to attend to it. First, it's a soft voice that we don't hear and keep forcing. Then it turns into a desperate cry. To love is to care and to care is to love. This is my mantra.

I can

I meditate every morning and every night religiously without exception because I need it. A healthy and conscious diet, and choose my peace above all things. Manage moments of uncertainty, anxiety, fears, and limiting beliefs to transform them into confidence, security, joy, empowerment, and strength, recovering and acknowledging my value, remembering all the way I have traveled, and my ability to love in extreme circumstances knowing that I am brave.

I do everything I want even if they are great challenges and carry them out. I am living in the full extent of the word and living in capital letters. Life is a gift. Life is today; life is now.

Every Day a New Dawn

My recommendations are to meditate, laugh, have positive thoughts, and create affirmations of love and share them with our loved ones.

These four steps have been fundamental in giving me inner strength, calm, confidence, and hope. I take care of my internal dialogue so that it is loving and constructive, do not feel it is a struggle but rather a surrender, it feels that I am being rocked by the waves in the sea, seeing a beautiful blue sky and feeling the caress of the sun on my skin. The flow embraces the best of me, and my emotions and thoughts can be like a lifeline of healing if they harbor hope and love.

Love Without Measure

Come Back To Me
Still today I apologize because I suspend learning with myself again. Circumstances and life pushed me then and I continue to do so now.

I know that health is the most valuable thing we have, but when putting myself off is a habit, even being aware that this time my body said this far, I am slowly learning that I am my priority, here, today, and now. It is vitally important to forgive myself and to take care of myself since love begins with oneself. Allowing myself time and rest, knowing how to say no and not feeling bad about it, my peace is my anchor.

 All this set of acts with myself is the reflection of a new beginning.

Accept what each offers.
My love for my loved ones is great and deep, so I decided to wait until the last moment to communicate it just one weekend before starting the first phase of my chemotherapy treatment.

My sisters live 600 kilometers away and we made a video call before I was talking with my beloved God filling me with loving calm and inner strength. First, they got a little angry for having hidden it during those months, then they encouraged me telling me that everything would be fine, I know that they also made a great effort to find out about my condition.

My older sister came to accompany me for my second dose of chemotherapy and she came back again to see us before going into the operating room, there were still great restrictions in hospitals due to the pandemic, and in no way could she receive visitors.

My little sister traveled to join us once I was back home from the operation. My older sister stayed with me for a few more days until I was able to put my foot back on my toes with the help of crutches. I love hugs, and in those moments they were like vitamins for my soul, especially those of my daughter, I wanted to melt into them and treasure them inside my mind and heart.

Love Without Measure

Learning to Receive
In my experience and search, it has been important to know how to receive help. It has not been an easy exercise for me. I searched for information on natural and holistic medicine to alleviate the side effects of chemotherapy and radiotherapy.

During the process, an excellent doctor told me what natural products and food would help me. I searched for expert doctors who, in addition to traditional medicine, had implemented their research together with integrative medicine.

All this helped me immensely, knowing that I was giving my body the help it was going to need, extra help for the process and forever. Health is the biggest and best investment that we can give to our lives.

From the Spanish Cancer Association, I received psychological and financial support, both important, since it is not easy to feel understood in that sea of emotions that living each aspect of the disease means, and you can feel very alone.

Sowing Seeds of Love
I am fascinated by helping and offering encouragement to all people, some are friends, and others come by chance, although nothing is by chance, everything is casual.

During this time and with different diagnoses, I feel that I have been able to help several friends with words of encouragement, confidence, and always with good humor as I say.

Love Without Measure

Also offering them all my knowledge that is within my reach. It is fantastic to be able to offer and support each and every one of them. In my dreams, I always visualize a circle of women where I invite them to rediscover themselves through meditation, music, and dance, healing words and forming with them a necklace of sea shells that contain those wonderful pearls in which we are able to see all our greatness.

> *La vida es un tejido entre Dios y yo*
> *En cada momento del día,*
> *Dios empuja hacia abajo la aguja*
> *y yo la empujo hacia arriba... Así tejemos*

Accept whatever diagnosis it is, but never accept a prognosis. Never give up hope! Dance even with your mind, raise your eyes and look at the sun, you are light, we are light, surrender, surrender, and don't stop loving yourself. And as a poem says "dance as if no one was watching you.

***

Chapter 8

Move Your Body, Change Your Brain - Create a Powerful Positive Shift for Health, Happiness, and Joy

Dawn Gaden

Dawn Gaden

Self Image Expert

Brighton, MI USA
support@theimageshift.com

Move Your Body, Change Your Brain - Create a Powerful Positive Shift for Health, Happiness, and Joy

> 66 ——————
>
> *The words that empowered me to find my strength are "there's a power within me that's greater than anything I will ever encounter!"*

My name is Dawn Gaden. I help professional women get unstuck from limiting beliefs so they can rewire their brains for success with movement, mantras, and meditation to create lasting sustainable change and powerful positive self-images.

Dawn Gaden is the CEO of Mind Body Counseling and Coaching, an international speaker, and best selling author. Her global coaching program - The Image Shift - helps professional women get unstuck from limiting beliefs and rewire their brains for success. Dawn is a licensed counselor, self-image coach, Verified intenSati Leader, and Registered Yoga Teacher.

She shares her passion and knowledge of how beliefs change your biology and your brain with exercise and how mindfulness creates an empowered living.

Move Your Body, Change Your Brain - Create a Powerful Positive Shift for Health, Happiness, and Joy

Typical American Dream

I had it all - married, four amazing boys. Our youngest are twins - that was a beautiful surprise. We had a house in the woods to raise our four boys. Mike, my husband, worked full-time while I worked part-time as a licensed counselor and yoga teacher so that I could be home to raise our boys. It really was a perfect life. After the twins were born, we upgraded to the house in the woods - sorta outgrew the 3 bedroom ranch! Just like that, life was falling into place. And just as quickly, things began to fall apart. Along came the twins, we bought the dream home in the woods, and Mike lost his job. Fear set in and then came survival. I was really good at taking action, so I got a full-time job.

My Wakeup Call During a Dark Rainy Day

It was a dark rainy day as I ventured off to work. Terrified because all I wanted to do was escape my life, I had nothing left to give for me or my kids. I was depleted and exhausted. I prayed, "God, you have to give me something else; this I cannot handle". I truly believe God helped me wake up from my trance of unworthiness to take action to live my life again. Shortly after that, I began to notice large lumps in my groin area; they came and went. Until finally, they were not going anywhere, just kept growing bigger and bigger. After the biopsy that led to two fused lymph nodes being removed, I waited for the call. I was standing on my front porch, phone in hand. It was July 10, 2010. It was a sunny day, and my husband and I stood paralyzed on the porch as the phone rang. The voice says, "It's cancer". Just like that "it's cancer" in a tone you hear from someone ordering off a menu or reading from a list of items to purchase from the grocery store. Don't they realize they just said two words that will forever change my life and my family? Did I realize it? Not really. I hung up the phone, kissed my husband goodbye, and said softly, "We'll figure it out", and headed off to work. I went on autopilot, moving through my day and life as I was "supposed" to be — take care of the family, make the money, just do it. That was the inner voice. It was non-Hodgkin's lymphoma, follicular lymphoma to be exact, that turned all that around. I woke up, took charge, and began to live consciously in my life.

Move Your Body, Change Your Brain - Create a Powerful Positive Shift for Health, Happiness, and Joy

Always Have Hope; Take the Chance On YOU!

I knew I needed to leave my job, take time off to heal, and pause. But how? Mike was still unemployed. We had 4 boys to feed. We had a house. How on earth do I do that? Will I fail my family? Is this really the right decision? YES. I stopped working for 2 years.

I took time to rest, heal, play with my kids again, and love my life again. I had hope. I had the desire to be more than what my current situation was. I AM stronger than I think. I AM braver than I seem. I AM powerful beyond measure. I had to have faith, passion, and deep trust in my inner knowing (my connection to God) to know this was the way.

This is my advice to you. Believe in yourself. Wake up your heart, mind, and spirit to take the chance on you.

It's About Me! Take Life One Day at a Time!

I hadn't taken two years off work - ever! What on earth was I going to do? Well, heal, sleep, play, laugh more, and yes sleep more. I was refusing to accept defeat and really knew nothing about follicular lymphoma but never entered the thought of defeat.

I would find a way to make each day count, no matter what. I had to decide on a treatment. I am a natural girl. No sugar, vitamins, natural all the way. Hmmm, I had so many options thrown at me at one time. Chemo? Radiation? Surgery?

Wow! I had to really take a look at all my options and decide what would be the best course of action for me. It didn't matter what others did or thought. This was really about me. I had to decide. So I decided why not bump up the vitamins, healthy eating, and traditional medicine. I used my meditation every day. I practiced my intenSati (movement, mantras, meditation) every day, eating healthy. The list was long and did include antibody treatment, a round of radiation, and some chemo.

This all unfolded over a course of several years as follicular lymphoma likes to re-occur over time. I took it one day at a time and one moment at a time. As my wise mentor taught me, "1% improvement 1 day at a time!". Self-love is key!

I Am Strong! Choice Is My Superpower!

I was terrified. At first. Quit my job? No income! Four kids to feed - not just feed them but offer them a beautiful life with two present parents that could provide them support and strength. I took a huge risk to leave that job. But the other choice was to continue to destroy my happiness. I believe that I am here for a purpose. I have a mission, and I need to believe in it more than believe in my weakness and fear that I would be ok -no matter what the future holds because no one can predict the future. So I had to decide how to take my next step forward. And the key to life was happiness, joy, and fulfillment. As a therapist, I continue to see people give up six-figure incomes because they were depleted and empty. I continue to see that the key, my 'aha moment', was that happiness is the key and that I had to choose. My life is in my hands. I often say that 'choice is my superpower!' I get to decide each decision I make. And even more, I get to decide what I think, how I feel, and how I move forward in my life. Sure it's hard, so what! I remind myself I am stronger than the biggest struggle I encounter. And so are you!

My Voice is Medicine

For the longest time, I couldn't whisper the word 'cancer'. I didn't even tell my family when I was diagnosed. My mom was my messenger. I was the strong one. I was the one that helped others. I couldn't ask for help.

Frankly, I didn't even know how to receive help. That was my lesson in all of this. I had to experience my weakness and my vulnerability in order to learn to accept others and to be a part of my community in a real way, not just the helper, the fixer, the one that had all the answers. I now share my cancer story, not just to flex my muscle of vulnerability, but to also help others. I truly believe that my struggles and experiences are meant to be medicine for others. We are not alone on this planet - even when we feel like it. We are here to lift each other up. And I continue to do my work with clients, connect more

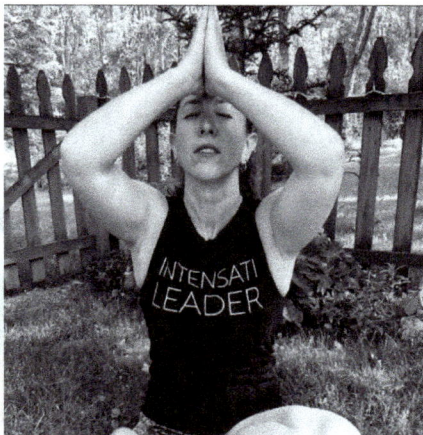

with family and friends, and continue to be authentic, live my truth, and take risks. And honestly, the biggest action I have taken is creating a 5 a.m. morning practice, 30 minutes of movement, usually intenSati, meditation, journaling, and intention setting for the day. It is my life raft!

Choice is a Superpower! Your Health is in Your Hands!
Know that your health is in your hands. You are hiring a medical, mental health, and wellness team. Find the experts that fit you. Make sure they have the knowledge and expertise, and of course, kind hearts to see you as a person. Ultimately, remember that you make the final decision. It is your life! Value yourself.

When I decided to choose chemo and other medical treatments, I had to make a conscious and heart decision to trust my choice and that whatever I put into my body will be used for healing. Fear was not an option. Doubt was not an option. Once I made a decision, I had to trust that it was for my best and highest good. I recommend the four steps below.

1. Your health is in your hands.
2. You hire your team.
3. You must trust yourself.
4. You must keep the power of a positive mindset.

Move Your Body, Change Your Brain - Create a Powerful Positive Shift for Health, Happiness, and Joy

Forgiveness is key. I use the Hawaiian forgiveness prayer - Ho'opono pono: I love you. I'm sorry. Please forgive me. Thank you. Kind words and self-talk are key. Our words have power, and they are like planting seeds. Make sure to plant seeds of love, joy, passion, and enthusiasm in the soil of your soul. IntenSati is the practice I used and then later became a verified leader to teach it.

This practice created magic for me in shifting my mindset, creating an elevated state of emotion, and moving my body in a strong powerful way. It fuels my soul every day. Find something that fuels your soul and do it every day! Rest. Stop doing so much and practice just being. I love meditation for this. It helps me slow down, calm down, and tune into my heart.

Family of Love

My family was amazing. I am grateful for their support even when I didn't want them to be a part of this. I didn't want to burden them with my problems. They were able to support me with love and action. I also did have to learn to ask for what I needed.

People don't always know what they need. Remember, no one knows how to read minds, even fellow cancer thrivers. So we have to use our voice and ask for help and support. It's true some people disappear and fall off the radar. It's ok. Cancer scares everyone. Just focus on those that are there for you. Show up with a loving heart.

Ask for Help

The Leukemia and Lymphoma Society offered free gifts for the kids at Christmas. I reached out to them from the hospital, and they offered the support they had. It was a lifesaver. Not only did this ease some financial burden, but they also shipped the box of gifts right to the house. It was a blessing. When I felt stable, I realized that maybe my kids could use support in ways I could not offer.

The cancer organization here in Ann Arbor offered a family event/program to help parents and kids through the cancer experience. It was such a valuable experience. I wanted to make sure my kids were getting what they needed and weren't overlooked during my struggle.

Move Your Body, Change Your Brain - Create a Powerful Positive Shift for Health, Happiness, and Joy

I Shine Brightly!

I am here for a purpose. Each and every one of us is. No matter how long we have been on this planet, none of us really know how important we are. We can make a difference. From a simple smile

to a stranger at the grocery store to running a non-profit organization, we can make a difference and create a brighter future for all. As a counselor and self-image coach, among many things, I had to learn how to serve others without losing myself. I continue to nurture my heart and soul with my practices while building a business that offers a new way of looking at life. When we change the way we look at things - the things we look at change. I think Wayne Dyer said that!

Continue to be the light for all to see. Ultimately, IntenSati is my legacy to teach and share with the world.

My favorite quote is from Deepak Chopra - It reminds me of my power to choose my thoughts.

❝ —

Every cell in your body is eavesdropping on every thought that you think

Laugh Your Heart Out!
You've got this! When I was in my darkest moments, I would watch a comedy. Laugh, just bring on that belly laugh until your pee moment. Get the happy hormones flowing through your veins. When I can't escape life, I go to my favorite beach in my mind. Remember the mind is so powerful.

Let's Connect!
https://dawngaden360.com/

Here is My Free Gift to YOU!

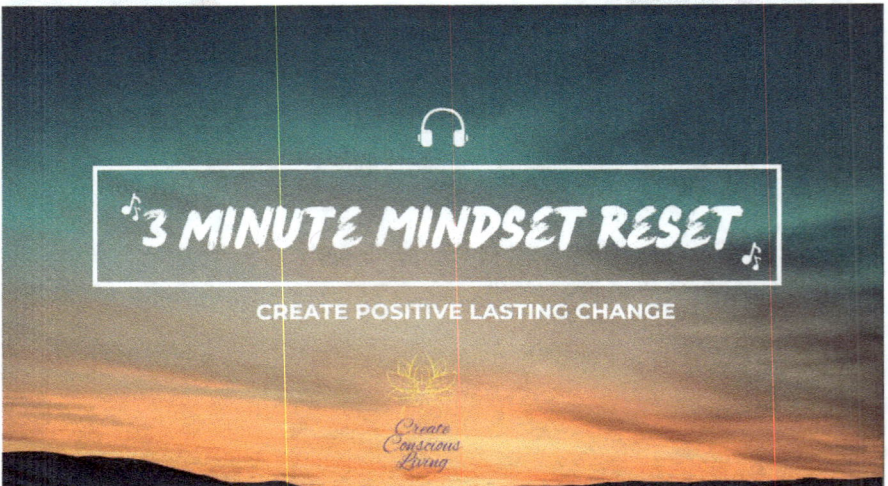

Chapter 9

Own Your Awesomeness
You Are Much More Than Your Illness!

Amelia Fjellvard

Amelia Fjellvard

The Queen of Joy

Larvik, Norway
post@ameliafjellvard.com

Own Your Awesomeness
You Are Much More Than Your Illness!

My name is Amelia Fjellvard. I help women unleash their power no matter the circumstances to regain their inner strength, peace, flow, and joy in the NOW.

My mission is to empower especially women to live with power, passion, and purpose - even in the face of hardship through dance and embodiment. I aim for people to stand firm and be connected with their authentic selves through self-care and self-love so they can own their AWESOMENESS.

Believe You Are Hot, Hot, Hot
Get your ass moving to some excellent music and look in the mirror while doing it! Tell yourself: Oh my…, I'm hot, hot, hot.
BELIEVE IT! You are so much more than your diagnosis.

Amelia empowers women from all walks of life to regain their inner strength, peace, flow, and joy in the NOW. Amelia is an expert and scholar who has researched and trained on a holistic view of health and well-being for more than 30 years.

She is also an international speaker and author who hosts worldwide retreats to awaken women's inner flame that lights all areas of their lives. Amelia uses a wide range of body-mind techniques, dance, and body movements and connects bodily states with emotional and cognitive elements through dance and body movement activations, forest baths, meditations, breath work, and energy work.

Amelia is all about discovering your personal awesomeness, where you stand in your power, purpose, and passion to create an extraordinary life you love. No excuses.

Do it with COURAGE, CONFIDENCE, and CHARISMA!

Own Your Awesomeness
You Are Much More Than Your Illness!

Life, Before Cancer
A considerable part of my pre-stage cervical cancer story is about what happened before my first experience with it.

You see, I was sexually, mentally, and emotionally abused for 15 years, and I went out into the big world totally broken at the age of 16.

Of course, that led to many other unhappy stories. Sadly, sexual abuse and violence in childhood can lead to lifelong health damage. It affects health later in life in a powerful way, both physically and psychologically.

Research shows that violence and sexual abuse are seven times more likely to cause depression later in life. It also poses a significant risk for other diseases, such as cardiovascular disease, infections, and cancer.

You can probably imagine why I am so grateful that I had dance and mindfulness in my life. Holistic health and wellness have always been of big importance, and I am so grateful for that-It saved me so I could choose myself on a larger scale later.

My choice of focusing on my overall health created a balance in me which gave me enough happiness, calmness, energy, and strength to face my traumas and eventually heal and transform. It also gave me the strength and positivity to deal with my C3 situation.

C3 - Courage, Confidence, Charisma
I had my first experience with cancer when I was 30 years old.
It was a pre-stage of cervical cancer, C3 (the most severe cell change before cancer). Luckily, I was able to turn my C3 story into courage, confidence, and charisma.

Cancer couldn't break me - it made me stronger!

Own Your Awesomeness
You Are Much More Than Your Illness!

I noticed a difference in my body early on thanks to my healthy living. I felt that something was off; even if I had been to the doctor a few months earlier for my yearly check-up, I went again, which was a blessing because they could remove the cell change before it became too severe. Ever since then, I've been taken care of with regular check-ups. When I was 40, I had my second surgery, where they removed most of the cervix. My last operation was 1.5 years ago, where they removed my uterus, fallopian tubes, and ovaries. I am 56 years old and still live with the HPV virus in my body. Twenty-six years with the word cancer hanging over me has created stress and unrest in my body. During these years, I have also lost my father, grandmother, boyfriend, and friends due to cancer. These are painful losses and a reminder of my own situation.

After my last operation, I felt tremendously fatigued; I lost my mojo completely. I stopped socializing, and yes, I felt less of a woman, less sexy. I lost myself for a while. The B12 injections I had taken for 18 years no longer worked. Thank God I had experienced firsthand how my thoughts, beliefs, and emotions affect my health, and more than ever, I work on myself -mind, heart, body, and soul.

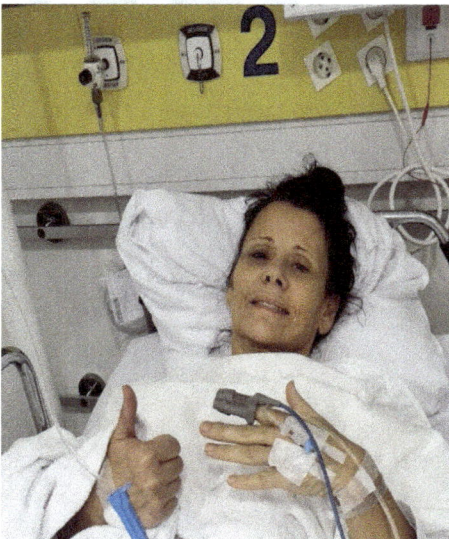

I can now say that I am more or less back to normal.

Here I am after my last surgery, showing some positive vibes giving thumbs up.

Overall, I've been lucky; I'm still here and never had to take chemotherapy or radiation. Living with the cancer threat and all the check-ups and operations have created stress in my system, but I know how to deal with that.

Own Your Awesomeness
You Are Much More Than Your Illness!

My situation would have been very different without systematic controls. In my country of Norway in 2021, 345 women got cervical cancer. The average age at diagnosis is 52 years. The disease is the ninth most common cancer among women, and 70 to 90 women die yearly. Thanks to the Norwegian healthcare system and myself, I'm still here, and I feel safe even if I still have the virus in my body. I'm convinced that we have more power to heal than we've been led to believe. We need to get to the root cause of the disease if we are going to find FREEDOM.

New ME Was Born - Danceology Inspiration
Cancer made me a better person. My perception changed, and the here and now became more important. I became more grateful for the "small" things in life—things like waking up to a new day, breathing, being able to walk, seeing, hearing, etc.

A new ME was born. I chose to work on ME holistically; mind, heart, body, and soul. I decided to have a positive attitude daily and was consistent with my morning routines. I chose to HEAL. I choose faith over fear every day.

I healed with nature, ate healthy foods and herbs, exercised, danced, and meditated - learned about energy healing and focused on a growth mindset. I became aware of my thoughts, beliefs, and emotions. I felt my feelings. Furthermore, I made sure to go out dancing with my friends. The people in my salsa community continuously bring me joy. While dancing, I get in touch with my sensuality and elegance. It makes me feel like a woman again.

My aha moment occurred during a speech I had in Paris a few months after my operation. While I was presenting my story of abuse and how I went from merely surviving to thriving, I recognized how strong I'd been and how far I'd come. I also saw how much my story affected and changed so many women that were listening to me.

Own Your Awesomeness
You Are Much More Than Your Illness!

There and then, I had an epiphany and I said to myself, *"You have come this far, girl. I am so proud of you. NOW, DO THE REST!"*
I knew I needed to become even more authentically me.
I'd not done fitness or dance for almost three years. I even stopped dancing. I had become non-social, had stopped feeling sexy, and had stopped dating. While talking to my audience, I just knew that I needed to come back to ME again. In my head, I was proud of how far I had come but at the same time had a new spark to do even better. There and then I made up my mind to level up, and even start dating again after 3 years of celibacy. I needed to get rid of some insecurities around men and put myself out there again. To honor myself I knew I had to get rid of my muscle tension syndrome in the pelvic floor, something that can happen after trauma, stress, or anxiety. When the muscle tension becomes too high, the blood flow becomes poorer, the muscles become stiffer and weaker, and over time they can become painful. I have learned that it helps to use some techniques where I alternate between tension and relaxation so I'm taking action and learning some great techniques that will heal this area. I'm way too young to lose my sexual mojo! That moment I chose ME again, and it felt AMAZING. I just knew that it would happen because I made up my mind.

Remember YOU always have a choice. Find your inner strength and just do it as I did. Yes, I fucking did it and so can you!!!

Here are some self-care tips that I always do to reconnect, realign, re-energize, heal, and transform:

Heal with Nature
While in nature, slow down, walk barefoot, relax, breathe, tune into your senses, observe, stay in the present moment, enjoy the stillness, meditate, and connect with mother earth and yourself. Tap into gratitude and just BE.

Own Your Awesomeness
You Are Much More Than Your Illness!

The Power of Dance
Dance to express yourself to heal. Dance for fun or dance your stress and illness away - even for brief moments. Dance or move to promote emotional, social, cognitive, and physical integration. Process, observe, assess, and intervene in your overall health through dance and body movement.

Tap into the Incredible Power of Breath
Become aware of your breathing. Breathe consciously and systematically and disconnect yourself from the mind and connect with your body and heart. Breathe through your thoughts, beliefs, memories, and actions that do not support your growth. Return to wholeness and make yourself more equipped to handle stressors around your illness.

The Timeless Benefits of Meditation
Refocus your attention on something calming like meditation. When we meditate, we calm our minds so the soul can speak. Become aware of your infinite potential, strength, love, and power.

Manage Your Energy
Understand how energy works and get your vitality back when you are drained, your health back when you are ill, and your joy when you are down. Outsmart stress and surrender to happiness. Surrender and instill strength, resilience, health, and vitality in your body.

Do you pause? Do you get a break from the hard stuff?
Do you practice any of the above so you can see the world from a new perspective, enjoy life, and have fun even in difficult times, even for some brief moments?

Healing Family Lineage
My family situation has been challenging due to everything that happened, so during the first years, I was a fighter and used to do everything myself so I just dealt with it!

Own Your Awesomeness
You Are Much More Than Your Illness!

However, when I came back to Norway due to cancer after many years in Spain, I knew that it was time to focus on healing myself completely so I could be strong enough to start healing my family.

It was time to stop the negative spiral, forgive, and let go.
Together we made it. Me taking the lead on the path to recovery and my family being open to going on the journey with me healed us all. We dared to do the work.

Today my family is very supportive, and I feel so grateful for having them in my life. I also have marvelous friends, and I know now that I will never have to deal with anything by myself again.

Connections—Are Everything
Make sure you have someone to talk to. Check your area regarding patient and peer organizations. They have often been through similar experiences and can contribute with their knowledge without you explaining everything. In Norway, we have The Cancer Association Counseling Service, which consists of cancer nurses and social workers who give advice and guidance; you should check and see if you have something similar in your area. It is also a good idea to search for various courses and meeting places. Maybe you have a cancer coordinator and a cancer nurse in your area that can help you with what you need.

They can be helpful when it comes to getting help organizing appointments and dealing with your everyday life. More than anything, make sure to let your family and friends in. You don't have to and should not need to fight this battle alone.

I'm lucky because we have a great support system in Norway when it comes to patient rights, the economy, and practical help. My doctor, gynecologist, and hospital staff were incredible. Everyone informed me well. My questions and needs were met; they always made me feel seen and heard whenever I was afraid or sad. It made all the difference in the world - it made me feel safe and secure.

Own Your Awesomeness
You Are Much More Than Your Illness!

Leading, Living, and Leaving a Legacy

My path led me to help women that feel stressed, overwhelmed, fatigued, or burned out to find deep inner strength, peace, flow, and joy in the NOW, no matter their circumstances. I help women to discover how to authentically express themselves through activities like dancing, forest bathing, energy work, meditations, and breathwork. Reconnect, re-align, re-energize, heal, and transform.

Wouldn't it be lovely to find deep inner peace? A state of flow in your everyday life, filled with wonderful energy, lots of creativity, and joy? What if you could come back to yourself and fill up your own cup so you can burst with energy, joy, and love for life so you could appear as the beautiful, authentic, loving, and playful person you really are? How would that feel?

Whatever you have endured, REMEMBER:

66——

You are not your circumstances. You are your possibilities. If you know that, you can do anything.

- Oprah Winfrey

Own Your Awesomeness
You Are Much More Than Your Illness!

Because You Deserve It!

I would LOVE to give you a free 30-minute class where I show you a morning routine that will make your body and mind strong and healthy.
I will guide you through movement, breathwork, and meditation.
You will love this routine; that's a promise.

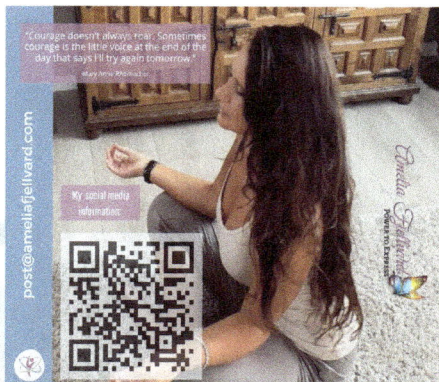

Reach out to one of my social media platforms mentioned above. I look forward to talking with you.

Inner Flow of Joy

My second gift to you is to give you access to my free "Inner flow of Joy" 3-Online Video Series, an ultimate solution that will transform your life and business.

May you be blessed with peace, love, and wisdom!

Chapter 10

Seeing the Light Through the Darkness

Jorge Manuel Vasquez

Jorge Manuel Vasquez, Jr.

Co-Founder of Vasquez Jiu-Jitsu Academy

Arlington, Tx, USA

jvasquez4200@gmail.com

Seeing the Light Through the Darkness

Jorge Vasquez is a Brazilian Jiu-Jitsu black belt, a Pan American Champion, a Kasai Pro Fight winner, Fight2Win Veteran, and a multiple-time IBJJF gold medalist. Sports have always been his passion; he uses sports to help him relieve stress, anxiety, and other emotions. Jiu-Jitsu has helped him accomplish many things off and on the mat such as self-discipline, commitment, and perseverance. He is a co-founder of Vasquez Jiu Jitsu Academy. My mom is Angelica Benavides, and you will read her chapter later in this book.

Growing Up

Growing up, my life before my mom had cancer was pretty normal. I played sports, hung out with my friends, and spent time with my large family. When my mom and my dad got divorced when I was six years old, we moved from Laredo, Texas to Dallas- Fort Worth.

I always strived to be a good student, but traditional schooling was not suited to the way I wanted to learn. So I ended up being homeschooled towards the end of high school. My whole life I consider myself to be a silly person and an extrovert. I have a tendency to make people laugh because it makes me happy. Too.

Reality Kicks In

My mom having cancer affected me in many ways both negatively and positively. It was a very stressful, scary, and unpredictable time not knowing what was going to happen next. We were practically living day by day. Although my mom having cancer created a lot of uncertainty, it brought me, my mom, my brother, and my extended family closer together.

118

Seeing the Light Through the Darkness

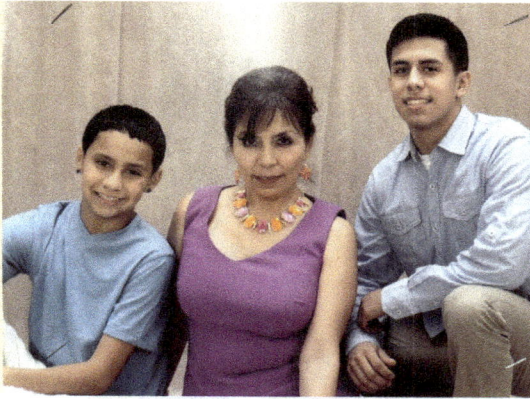

What I love most about the experience is that it taught me how to deal with uncertainties and difficult moments in my life.

I am not much of a storyteller, but I am always kidding around with my mom telling her, she is a hippie.

She is very intuitive and suspected something was wrong with one of her breasts.
Just the thought of her suspecting something was wrong was scary, but I didn't think much of it. She finally made a decision to get checked. What the heck, I thought. I was in shock at the thought of my mom having cancer. The day I didn't

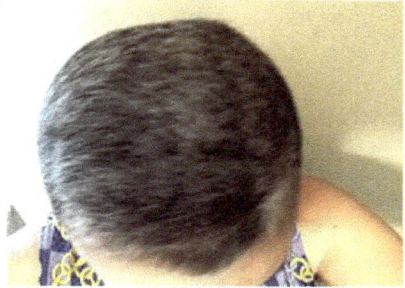

want to come finally approached me; she came into my room and told me that she in fact did have breast cancer.

At that moment I was in disbelief. It really started to hit me once all her treatments started, her surgeries began, and she lost her hair. In fact, I bald my hair to support my mom and bald her hair. As time went on, it became more real.After my mom's diagnosis, I started to focus on what I can and can't control because my mom's health, for the most part, was out of my control. I could control how I was available for her and how I could handle my anxieties by telling myself to live in the moment. Being able to take control of my thought because I didn't want to give her another thing to worry about when she was already going through enough was necessary.

Make Every Moment Count
As children of cancer patients, we also experience dark moments during these difficult times. Many times, I would come home late from work and would sit by my mom's bed. I felt that I just had to enjoy these simple moments in the event that she did end up not beating cancer.

Seeing the Light Through the Darkness

I wanted to make sure I was there for her and help her instead of trying to be consoled because I was so sad. I had to just remain strong and grateful when I was there by her side.

People going through cancer already have a full plate, and our job should make their treatments and processes as easy as possible. We don't want to bring negative thoughts and negative talk around them. We also don't want to tell them how bad we feel about what they're going through because, in the end, they're the ones going through it. The best thing we could do for them is to be there to help them up

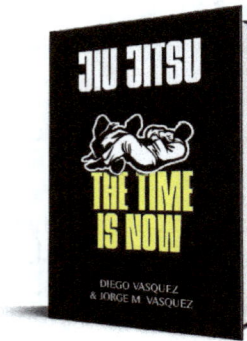

when they're feeling down. Even though this is also a difficult time for you, it will really make a difference in changing the way we think and support them. Being able to support our family members during this time will help them get through these dark moments. You have to hold on to the belief that they will heal. During these dark moments, it's a test to really believe in yourself and trust in the process.

You will be okay. At the time, I would journal and write down exactly my feelings. I would just journal and just take it day by day. I highly recommend you do the same; that is my biggest piece of advice. My brother and I created our first Jiu-Jitsu notebook if you want to get it on Amazon to journal your emotions.

Facing Mortality in Life

In addition to journaling which was part of my healing process, the other step in the healing journey is learning to accept death. It will happen to all of us. Everything has a beginning and end.

Seeing the Light Through the Darkness

This is the most real thing about life, but we all avoid the word itself. Those people experiencing cancer deal with the thought, and it seems to be right there in their faces. You can hide from it; you can avoid it. The real healing was I had to face a fear of mortality of my own death and my loved one's death and really work on that aspect of my life. Ever since then, I feel as if I can process people's death or people's sorrows better because I had to face so it's not a foreign challenge to me because eventually in the future, it's something I'll have to deal with again. I was able to learn what the darkest moments of my life today feel like, and I can prepare for when it does happen again.

Now everyone must try everything possible to heal. There is a holistic approach and Western Medicine Approach. I would say you don't ignore one or the other. If possible, I would say you could do both. Do everything you can but don't try to get stuck on one way like I only want to do holistic or I don't want to do Western medicine. I would say if you can do it all, do it. Give yourself a better chance but don't get single-track-minded. Pick your best medicine to heal. There is no one way of tackling cancer. So if you can get all the weapons—metaphorically speaking necessary to fight cancer, then the chances of your healing are better. I don't believe there is one magic bullet to heal. I just believe both Western medicine and alternative medicine are a great combination. My mom used both. Everyone has their own medicine bag they like and trust. She grabbed the bull by its horns to heal and find happiness.

Witnessing All the Helping Hands

My big Aha Moment was discovering and witnessing people you never expected to be there for you were there for us. Watching and witnessing people show up in so many ways was amazing. My brother and I were very young so getting support from many people felt great. I felt we were not alone. Even if you don't know someone personally who can really help you get through these dark times, find a community or someone to talk them.There are good people in this world. My aunts Blanca and Lourdes were always there for my mom, me, and my brother.

Seeing the Light Through the Darkness

The other Aha Moment that I had was when I felt sad and afraid because I realized my mom was trying to pick me up spiritually and emotionally. She helped me get through my difficult moments but I was like, wait that's not supposed to be this way. I'm supposed to help and be the person who lifts her spirit. I had to shift the way I was seeing things and not just making it about me. It was about me learning to help my mom; it became a big deal. I've always carried that through. When someone has cancer, I always remind someone that's going through something like that, that you're there for them. They're not there. They're not happy. They're not there to console you even though you might need help in shifting your mindset.

Avoid stressing your loved one — don't give them something more to deal with that they're already going through. They have you have a full plate.

Let us help them make their treatments and processes as easy as possible. Don't bring negative thoughts and negative talk around them.

Don't tell them how bad you feel about what they're going through. Find a counselor, friend, or community to talk to even though it might be a struggle for you. That's what's really gonna make a difference in the whole process, whether good or bad. Make sure you pick the right

support that will give you long lasting fruits of love,joy,and hope to keep going no matter how difficult life gets. At the end of the journey, it is all a life experience that shapes and makes you the stronger version of yourself!

Seeing the Light Through the Darkness

4 Steps Cancer Patients Can Use To Play The Game Of Life During Difficult Moments

The four steps I highly recommend are the following: First of all the main one is to stick together. Your loved one needs you and as much support as they can get. Stick to them through "thin or thick". My brother Diego and I grew closer together. We have each other's back! Diego is my young brother and he supports and lifts me even during triumph times.

Don't shy away from them or avoid them even if it brings anxiety or sadness. Secondly, you will be there not just for emotional support but physical. You might need to support them with doing chores, cooking, driving them to chemo or radiation, or simply sitting to talk to them. Third, I would say make the process easier by having fun or doing things you didn't do before maybe you can take a trip with them.

One of my favorite trips was when I proposed to my wife Ashley. My mom came with us to Peru where we hiking for 5 days to Machu Picchu. It was the most difficult hike but the most memorable experience.

My mom is an ordained minister. I was blessed to have her marry me and my beautiful wife Ashley. We now have a beautiful baby named Maxine Lola who is our love and joy.

If they are able to travel, make it happen. Make it a silly time and have a good time with them. The reality of cancer is they might make it and they might not make it.

Seeing the Light Through the Darkness

Make sure to take a lot of pictures, and videos, and create memories. One other thing I do in the month of October is wear pink clothes. My passion is Jiu-Jitsu and soon will open my own academy with my brother.

I wear pink spats, you know under my legs. You incorporate awareness during October to help other women to go get checked. Saving lives is key.

Self Love Acts

It is important to practice self-love, especially during those times. Remind your loved one to practice self-love, too. My mom knew she was going to lose her hair so she started looking for wigs and hats to wear. It was difficult, but it was fun for her at the same time. She now loves hair extensions. Make sure to dress up and put on makeup if you are a female. Go get pedicures and your nails done. Pamper yourself in many ways. Her friends cheered her up by wearing one of her wings during breast cancer month.

Look if you want to buy some things such as a dog, purse, or something you have been wanting, go buy it. Don't limit yourself. I am not saying to empty your bank account. I truly believe this is an act of self-love, in my opinion.

Seeing the Light Through the Darkness

If you want a nice car, and it is not in your budget, get a plan in place. Start saving money towards your goal. Tell yourself you're worthy of getting want you want. The other magic bullet is feeling loved by your partner, co-workers, or people around you. Just because you have cancer doesn't feel you're less. Step into your best version of yourself and step into loving and living the life you want. Life is too short. Love yourself and go after what you want.

One of the things I admire about my mom is that she achieves almost anything she sets her mind to. She is now dancing the bachata and salsa. She has now gained confidence again to start dating. My mom has broken away from limiting beliefs such as not feeling pretty or sexy

which became really big barriers both emotional and mental barriers because of her double mastectomy. Going through all her surgeries and body dysmorphia issues that cancer patients go through is a big deal, especially for women. She was able to break through because of practicing self-love and working on her appearance.

My way of practicing self-love is by doing what I am passionate about; that is Jiu Jitsu. My goal is to win as many gold medals. I know that with all the wins many failures will also come. Self-love means pushing through and not quitting but pushing through. I know I'll reach my goals which also include having my own gym. One thing I know for sure is that all my failures or potential headaches are minuscule compared to those battling for their life.

Seeing the Light Through the Darkness

Family Support

If you or a loved one is struggling with the idea of possibly losing their life or losing a family member. I strongly suggest talking to a counselor therapist, friends, and family. You might be feeling fear, doubt, and concern about losing your loved one. Find some type of support.

The truth is there were times when I felt sad, afraid, and uncertain. My mom was trying to pick me up and help me get through these difficult times. I was like, wait, that's not how I'm supposed to be. I'm supposed to help her get through these tough times. I needed to look at this from a different perspective. It's not about me. It's about me helping my mom. So that was a big deal for me at the time. I gained the strength and courage to deal with and find solutions instead of just feeling sorry for myself.

Now, I carry this wisdom that led me through dark moments to encourage others in similar situations. I always remind those going through these challenges that the only shortcut in life is that we have so much life in us. We must exchange energy, joy, and love with those going through cancer.

When someone is personally going through cancer, it's hard to tell them what to do because I didn't have cancer, but I can speak from firsthand experience. And it's the same thing I've said before, it's our job as children not to be consoled but to look for support such as counseling, friends, or an adult to vent with.

We must find ways to console and pick them up. Reassure them that you're going to be there for them and remind them that you love them and that things are going to be okay. If things don't turn out okay, have no regrets.

Seeing the Light Through the Darkness

Outside Support

Based on my experience, I would say the whole breast cancer medical field is super supportive. Everyone involved is hospital staff, chemotherapy staff, and the Cancer Association Services is awesome. They are very nice, kind, and helpful. They helped us feel calm and relaxed. All the people involved have big hearts and are available to do anything they can to help.

You don't have to grow your hair out you and don't have to donate money. You could do simple things. You can become a cancer buddy and just talk to cancer patients. You could make blankets and or pillows. My mom received several gifts. There are all kinds of ways to help, but I think everybody involved in the cancer medical field is awesome.

Well, in the past two years due to COVID-19 I haven't taken the initiative to be active for cancer patients. Before COVID, we would do a cancer walk for about three years straight in Dallas, Texas. I plan to do the walkathon next year again.

I would also like to find a family that is going through what we went through during my mom having cancer. I want to donate gifts for Christmas. It is time to pay it forward. One Christmas, we received many gifts from a couple. My mom was going through cancer and financial hardship. Receiving those gifts was a pretty big deal to us. It wasn't the gifts themselves, but the gesture and generosity. It was a great experience.

My last words of encouragement and final advice is never to lose hope. Even during the last minute, don't give up or stop fighting. My mom was in and out of the hospital for about 4 or 5 years including ICU. Don't stop believing and don't stop loving them! You know you can love even at your darkest times. Love will push you through whether that be a dog, baby, or adult just love especially when you are feeling down. Watch something funny, read, and tell jokes (TV, cartoons, movies) to help them come back to life. I will say it again, "don't give up hope; don't stop loving!"

Seeing the Light Through the Darkness

Living and Leaving a Legacy

I definitely believe that life is tough. Life can be hard, but never give up or stop progressing toward goals. You might not reach all the goals you set for yourself. However, I strongly believe that if we have hard challenging times, let's make it worth living by living and leaving a legacy as my mom says. Never give up no matter how difficult the situation may be. I always keep moving forward. I figure out solutions.

I might not find them right away but learning from these hard times is crucial. Most importantly, telling our story and sharing our message on how we overcame it is helpful. I always reached new and ambitious goals that are challenging. I also want to challenge those around me.

The other legacy that I want to leave behind is to learn about, live, and leave unconditional love behind. Love everyone no matter what they are going through, no matter what kind of people they are. Unconditional Love is key. These life principles are a huge part of my mom's legacy.

She has unconditional love for everyone that includes difficult people. She has a heart of gold. She was devoted to finding solutions, interventions, and curricula for special education students for more than 26 years. She has offered our home to many family members, a few crazy roommates, some friends who were homeless for a couple of weeks, and people on the street. She is always helping people which is a huge part of her legacy.

Her legacy is my legacy. I want to set goals like her. Every challenge she encounters becomes a goal where she finds solutions not only for herself but to share with others. She wants to inspire and motivate people to never give up no matter what. Not sure who said, "turn your mess into your message, 'GMA' Co-Anchor Robin Roberts". I want to do the same. I want to duplicate her passion and vision. My life goal is never to stop moving forward no matter what kind of obstacles life gives me.

I want to pass this on to my daughter, other children I may have, and generations to come. I also want to be known as my mom, "Ultimate Legacy Builder" focused on leaving and tapping into unconditional love.

Now, do you feel that after cancer? Maybe you and your loved one have reached more goals after having cancer because it created more momentum.

Journal Offer

Chapter 11

THE AHA DIARY

Helen Argyrou

Helen Argyrou
Visionary Drummer Psychologist
Limassol, Cyprus
druminspire@gmail.com

I elevate the credibility and authority of speakers, pioneers, and leaders to present their innovative thought leadership to global audiences, especially in the European sector and Exotic world locations.

Cancer is like an unwanted guest that finally leaves, gets back on the road again, once you realize the enlightening wisdom he/she dropped into you and your life.

A Hardening Ambition

I was a driven, powerful, and dynamic person, chasing my fate in over 13 countries around the world where I ran a unique series of drum workshops. I was an innovator and devoted change agent

for people and their causes. I developed a special style of sacred sound and drum therapy called Druminspire. Using this method, people became inspired to learn to build and benefit from collective action with the consensus of the group.I hosted drum orchestra events,always with a deep

WOMEN OF TRUTH
International
CONFERENCES RETREATS & BUSINESS EXPOS

VISIBILITY PUBLICITY AUTHORITY CREDIBILITY

psychological message about personal power. I was on my spiritual path, working as a yoga teacher, therapist and mediator for many years. Probably at times delusional, though very passionate, I had many desires for my life and believed I need to make our own destiny.

A Hand Awakened Me

I woke up one morning in August 2016 and found a hand pointing to my chest. As I came to, I realized this was my hand, and it was angled in such a way that it was pointing toward the crescent of my right breast. Only the crescent shape was angular - not rounded- which caused some concern. I discovered a lump and two weeks later a doctor confirmed cancer. It took another two weeks for me to tell anyone since my sister had just had breast cancer stage 4 three years before that.

I struggled to accept that my family would go through this all again with me and that I would actually have to endure the saga now myself. The positive estrogen hormone type breast cancer stage 2 diagnosis caused a month-long deliberation.   I decided to refuse chemo and have a mastectomy. This very conflicting decision felt as if I was agreeing to massacre

my own body despite my knowledge of tumor shrinking with natural methods. I had numerous 'downloads' about illness, the healthcare system and causes of toxicity. A deeply spiritual journey housed in an existential crisis began and only softened in the last months of 2022.

Quarantine and lockdown reminded me of the deep internalization of my recovery journey. I felt I could help others navigate covid because of my experience. I learned how to detoxify, adjust my relationships, change career, and get really honest with myself.

The one thing that outshined all this though was my deep connection with the divine feminine and yin energy that started overtaking my life. I realized how I carried so much fear from my conservative society and began confronting the self sabotage that had devastating effect. Most of all, I discovered the deep knowing that I would use all I learned and now know to serve others again in a new way.

Saying "Se la vie" … saying "Adieu"
After healing from that time in my life, so many things have been reshuffled, so much dust has finally settled and much cleaned out.. It all needed to go in stages and there are still some new ideas and outcomes to appreciate and implement. It can't all go at once. There is much of this that is a harrowing, tough, and harsh reality — from the physical to the psychological adjustments along with various specific attitudes and actions that must change. One major theme is about saying goodbye to what hurts, saying "Se la vie"… saying "Adieu"!

THE AHA DIARY

Throwing out old patterns - or 'the devil' off our backs- is a profound experience. It requires the castle or house of cards we built over years to come tumbling down. There are also some serious and real parts of who we once were, that also need to go, and it can feel harsh and unruly. Hancock's research explains that cancer is internal suicide, wrapped in denial.

Cracking the code of denial comes in the cancer journey, one of our darkest nights of our soul- where we fight to see the light we never could. To break through into deeper levels of truth and honesty with ourselves, to truly see ourselves beyond that veil, beyond our house of cards.

Obviously to confront darkness in places we never knew existed is grueling. It is also primordial and profound, as I said, because it is only by force with a cancer diagnosis for example that we begin to see what we could not and see anew what we can only now.

A Harrowing Adieu
Afterlife and Awakenings. Past lives and Power. Paradoxical emotions -which others blamed on the anesthesia- rocked my world. After my surgery, I remember feeling 'high' on the relief in the hospital room. Days later the 'fresh' prana of living clashed against strange downloads of female Amazonians from antiquity who cut off their breasts and priestesses burned for their spiritual magic. The aeons of suffering of the feminine essence demystified inside my desperate attempt to reconcile my life losing control with the hardest decision I ever made.

To dismember my body, my femininity... for my own good was beyond confusing.

THE AHA DIARY

Heavily prompted by Dr. Hancock's breast cancer patient profile, I realized my pain went deeper since I did not fit typical people pleaser types. My self-sacrifice was programmed, justified and accidental.

A therapist empath convincing herself to live life on her own terms but still 'tricked' into self abandoning. Karma, Dharma, or Drama became one thing as I began to answer the harshest question I ever asked myself. What is hidden in you that has caused this inner suicidal plan to self-destruct?

That spawned a five-year plan that removed and reworked many life convictions in which I often over gave. Finally at the end of that plan, I drafted a new career distinction that to no longer carries the weight of people's problems I own the responsibility of myself as a magical healer. To care for self before others for me means to no longer throw my pearls before swine.

Arrive Healthy Anew
-Although this journey is like climbing the rockiest mountainscape,…remember to return to kindness, softness, and the gentle side of living as often as you can. Like the view at the top of the mountain walk, it will bring a totally new perspective to you and others and how you live your life. You will see things only those who alk the path and observe from far away can witness.

-Give yourself all the time you need to heal but don't get too close to the idea of being a victim of this illness and never for too long.

-Start to practice every day with a commitment to get stronger and to Love yourself first and then others. Do this without sabotaging the love people offer you even if they haven't and will never know your pain.

-Never forget who you were before you got sick. Call that part of your soul back when you start feeling better. Love that part more.

THE AHA DIARY

Awareness Harmony Activation
1. Learn all you can about this illness; the way to heal. Find which pathway deeply resonates with you and chose that.
2. Believe you will attract the right people to help your healing and recovery; hang in there; they will come.
3. Start detoxing your life from pain, resentment, judgment, and any activities that you have become accustomed to that are not serving you at the deepest level.
4. Have and build the courage daily to choose again if it is a new career, relationship, country, or car... whatever you can refresh and renew, do this!

Another Helpful AHA List
1. Throw off any and all judgments or projections others had about you that may have hurt or affected you negatively.
2. While caring for others in relationships and friendships, develop boundaries in your need to be seen, heard, or understood by those who cannot from now on.
3. Start to examine and define your limits, gauge your desire for change carefully, and your tolerance levels and act accordingly.

Always Helpful Argyrous
*My family - the Argyrous - were very surprised I got sick since I was always so pedantic about health and wellness. It seemed ironic, confirming the unpredictability of the disease and how we underestimate it. Crossing continents they came to host me, cook for me, and drove me to the doctor's appointments during my mastectomy.

My mother was like the rock of Aphrodite, which is actually her name - insisting she book 10 hair appointments so I could get pampered while healing and circumvent the challenge of hand raising above my head.

My sister and family kept reminding me of love and union with weekly dinners. Keeping the family vibes strong and consistent was so helpful for me so I could have company and regular drop-bys later. Even when I got better, regular weekly/ biweekly dinners with or without stayovers made such a difference.

A Helpful Aunty
- An aunty can be very helpful at this time. Do you have one? Mothers may feel really sad and are possibly going to be doing or caring in specific ways, so an aunt can offer something unique. Mine helped me through my second phase of surgeries while we cried, we loved, laughed, and learned. She cooked more vegan-type rice, pancakes, and eggs benedict for her niece patient. This was part of my Priceless Recovery!
- Find a community-based women's group in your area and if possible one with women who have similar health issues and another with women who do not.
- Feed the healing and bonding in your family, that can happen at this time, with as much positivity and respect as possible. It is an invaluable time to heal and even forget vast past difficulties or misunderstandings.

Deep Healing Journey

I have begun to infuse more of my healing journey and all its beautiful insights into and throughout my work with women to raise their visibility in the world — to teach more considered boundary definitions and ways to

stop minimizing, forgetting, and diffusing our power and the self-abandoning that strengthens that. Mostly through my deepened respect and love for life - which trickled in droplets only sometimes and downpoured at others - I have absorbed the learning as a precious time that connected me primordially to the divine feminine principle and the journey we are all on to become more truthful to ourselves.

> ## *You are who you have been waiting for!*
>
> *Helen Argyrou*

Everything in life can turn into an opportunity. Don't force it though; just gently remember this, and the time will come when all the pain becomes transmuted into powerful teaching as nothing else could ever give you. It is pure alchemy, and you are the alchemist of your own life, your own shaman!

Please provide your Linktree or Blinq with all your social media information: Facebook, Instagram, Twitter, LinkedIn and Clubhouse
https://linktr.ee/helenaha

What's your free offer for cancer patients?
DIVINE POWER
A healing sound meditation - https://vimeo.com/390319099

Chapter 12

Transform Your Fear Into Your Power To Heal.

Ewa Andrykiewicz Zmyslona

Ewa Andrykiewicz Zmyslona

Creator of Overcome Fear to Heal program, Author and Mindset Coach

Brussels, Belgium

info@ewazmyslona.com

Transform Your Fear Into Your Power To Heal

My name is Ewa Andrykiewicz Zmyslona. I help cancer patients and their families to overcome fear to heal and activate their Super Powers.

Dear Friend,

Please find a poem that I wrote to myself at the moment when I had to face my healing journey:

Beloved

I am really sorry that you have to go through this.
I deeply appreciate your strength and perseverance.
I love you so much.

I don't know how it ends.
But I know I will always be with you.
I love you so much.
Love is the strongest Power, the Power of God
that fulfills me.
I am learning to trust this power, this Love,
to be able to go through this path.

I called my soul for help.

Transform Your Fear Into Your Power To Heal

Ewa Andrykiewicz Zmyslona healed using a combination of traditional and mindset/energy therapies. While accepting the advice of doctors, she took her healing into her own hands as well, focusing on her body's ability to heal, the life she wanted ahead of her, and the belief that she had the ability to create her future as desired.

A skilled life coach with MBA and a background in science and project management, Ewa has used her exceptional human skills to help clients achieve success for many years. Now her focus and intention is to give others a place where they will feel loved, cared for, and supported on their own healing journey and activate their own superpowers. She is the founder of the Overcoming your fear to Heal program for cancer patients and their families.

How it all started...
Peacefully lying in bed, I suddenly started to feel pain in my belly. As a mother, I knew the pain, but this time it felt different. I knew that I wouldn't be able to take it much longer. I called my husband to ask him to call an ambulance. I started vomiting. My body wasn't able to take the pain any longer. I needed help now.

Then, as I was sitting and waiting to go to the hospital, I saw a vertical light on the right side of me, and I heard very clearly,

❝ ━━━━

Everything will be okay! everything will be okay! everything will be okay.

Transform Your Fear Into Your Power To Heal

I went to a hospital with an ambulance and 2 hours later had an emergency operation.

During my healing journey, I decided to take advantage of the power of defining my own story, expressing what had happened to me and what it meant.

Describing My Own Story
How did I see myself? What story did I tell myself? How would I define the most important story of my life? Would it empower me or disempower me? I started with self-compassion.

My ovarian cancer healing journey took place in 2018.

> *I Call My Soul*
> *"I am a channel of Grace. "*
>
> *- Saint Teresa of Ávila*

I was listening to the audiobook from Caroline Myss "Entering the Castle", about Saint Teresa of Ávila over and over again.

There is a calling "to represent an invisible power in the world through personal spiritual practice, through the power of prayer, though living

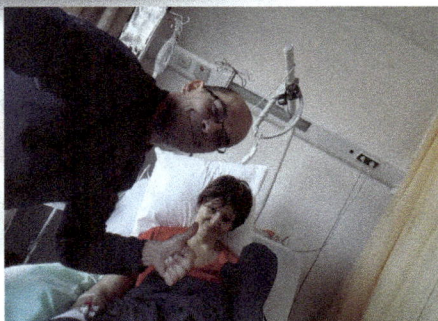

consciously and practicing compassion, and through becoming a channel for grace."

Recognizing myself as a channel of grace in this challenging period was one of the most important decisions I have taken. Little did I know then how much impact my journey would have. It created a ripple effect on myself and the people around me. Strangely enough, my soul knew.

Transform Your Fear Into Your Power To Heal

And you know what?
> *Accept it.*
> *You are important.*
> *You are Love.*
> *You are Powerful beyond your understanding.*
> *Become empowered!*

66 ——

Health and Healing are not about health and healing. It's about you becoming empowered with your own power."

- C.Myss

I Am Invincible

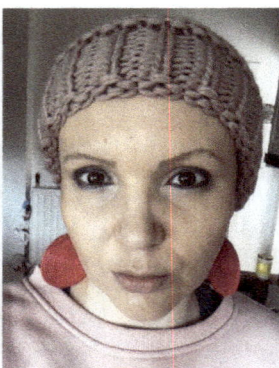

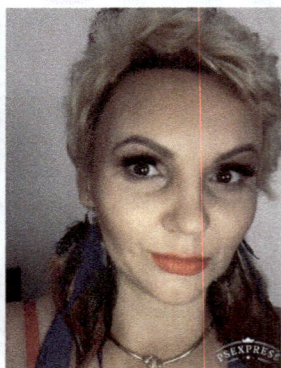

66 ——

You never know how strong you are until being strong is the only choice you have.

Bob Marley

Transform Your Fear Into Your Power To Heal

On a rainy November day, I met with my doctor to discuss the results of my long journey of healing from ovarian and endometrial cancer: the chemotherapy and the two operations I went through.

Expecting the final happy ending after the difficult chapters were over, we sat down in a small room with the three of us. Only a small desk separated us. The doctor started to speak; he was very calm, and he went straight to the point. The CT scan showed multiple areas of spreading cancer in the lungs and other areas. "Scattered lung nodules growing in size and a number of right hilar ganglion passing from 12 to 14 mm increase in the size of the inguinal lymph nodes."

Silence entered the room for a moment or two.
Then he started to talk and talk... about something. But I couldn't hear anything.

My body completely shut down.
For me, it was like, "What? Wait, What?"
I didn't understand.
It must have been a mistake.

"There are other solutions." He started to explain what we should do next, but I was still in shock, "Wait, What?"

"I've executed the plan perfectly. What are you talking about?" I thought.

"The chemotherapy did not work?" I naively asked. "Really? Didn't it?"
"Wait, what?"
My doctor tried to explain my situation and what my options were. I left his office.

        ...
Am I dying?
Because I'm not supposed to. Is God informed?

Transform Your Fear Into Your Power To Heal

Later I was connected by a friend to Suzanne Clegg, who works with cancer patients through the Image Cycling method. Meanwhile, I had a PET scan.

And the results stated:
"You still have nodules, the spots we see on the scan, but from the PET, we know that you have no cancer cells."
I must admit I was quite shocked. I didn't expect that.
"No cancer?" "No cancer, wow."
I'm healed.

My biggest aha moment is the realization that - **I Am The Boss of My Health! And I am not a victim!**

Yes, I get that we would all prefer a magic pill.

There is one - YOU!

You empower yourself thanks to your ability to decide what's best for you.

You are Not a VICTIM!

Do you know how to become the Boss of your life and health? This amazing concept of taking ownership of your life, being the BOSS of your life and health, is one of your greatest powers.

I wrote a book that became a bestseller! - "The Healing Mindset, How Cancer Activated My 8 Superpowers", Amazon 2020.

Transform Your Fear Into Your Power To Heal

You are Powerful!

I went through 8 Power activators during my healing journey:

1. I Am Invincible.
2. I Define My Own Story.
3. I Live By My Intuition.
4. I Am The Boss Of My Health - not a victim!
5. Transform Fear Into Love.
6. I Create My Own Support Team.
7. I Have The Power To Choose & Decide.
8. I Call My Soul.

As a support system, I recommend my book and my own online program that I share now with cancer patients and their families.

Overcome Fear to Heal

How can you benefit from this program?

1. Stop being terrified and move in the direction of healing.
2. Release the shock after a diagnosis and plan your next step.
3. Help someone you love and gift them this program, so you don't feel helpless.
4. Use the experience of others and know there are many solutions.
5. Prepare for different events during your treatment, so you know what to expect.
6. Choose your favorite methods of releasing stress and fear.
7. Stop isolating yourself and know there are many others in your situation.
8. Bounce back.
9. Bounce back again.
10. Activate new resources for your healing journey.

Transform Your Fear Into Your Power To Heal

Let's Connect:

Ewazmyslona.com

Ewazmyslona.com/course

info@ewazmyslona.com

I am following my heart, sharing love and blessing.

https://www.facebook.com/profile.php?id=1551166758

https://www.instagram.com/ewa_andrykiewicz_zmyslona/

Ewazmyslona.com

Free Gift:
ewazmyslona.com/gift

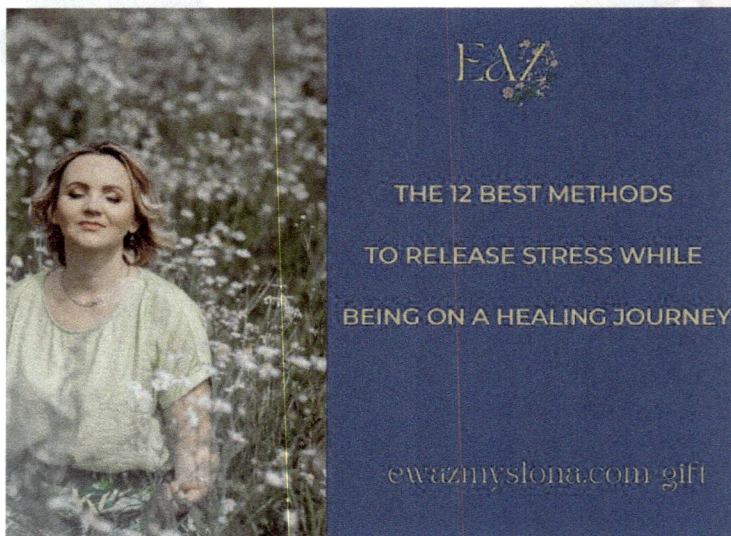

Chapter 13

You're Not Dead Yet... Get Up!

Dr. Michelle Mras

Dr. Michelle Mras

Speaker, Coach, Multi-Media Host

Colorado Springs, Colorado, USA

me@michellemras.com

Positive Cancer Message

Change is an emotional journey. It's not rainbows and butterflies in a field of daisies. Change is uncomfortable and forces you to evaluate who you are. The beauty is in the possibilities!

> *You are braver than you believe, stronger than you seem, and smarter than you think.*
>
> - A.A. Milne

I am a survivor of multiple life challenges. I guide others to recognize the innate gifts within them, stop apologizing for what they aren't, and step into who they truly are... Unapologetically.

I accomplish this through one-on-one and group Coaching, Training events, Keynote Speeches, my Books, Articles, and Podcasts.

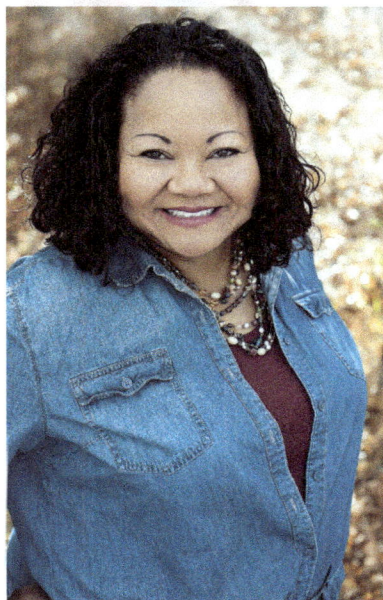

Michelle Mras, November 2017

Unintentional

Before cancer, I lived my life like a leaf on the wind without intentionality. I allowed things and people outside of me to sway my thoughts and behavior. I was simply living life. After cancer, I experience life and take great joy in the little things that occur every day. I break out in songs, normally Broadway tunes, at the drop of a hat. I smile at strangers and stop for children just to let them know they are AWESOME!

I dance in the rain and jump in mud puddles. Life is an adventure for me now. I enjoy every moment I have been blessed to have my eyes opened. I don't hold grudges and I rarely get upset. Life is far easier when it is full of joy and love.

You're Not Dead Yet... Get Up!

Trust Yourself

In early 2017, I requested to have bloodwork and a mammogram. Because of a previous condition, a traumatic brain injury from an auto accident, my concerns were dismissed. Finally, to calm my nerves, my primary care doctor submitted the requests for lab work and a mammogram.The lab work was clear. At my mammogram appointment, there were no lumps, but afterward, the technician

noticed that I was wiping up blood that had come out of my nipple. She brought in the Radiology doctor to examine me. He said he suspected a rare type of cancer called Paget's Disease of the Breast. He suggested I wait 30 days, then, if there was any change, I should go to my primary doctor immediately and get a biopsy.

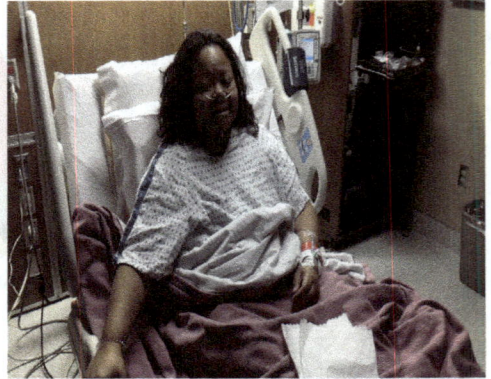

Within 20 days, there was a dramatic change to my areola. It took 30 days to get into an appointment to see a Nurse Practitioner. She examined my right breast and said, "That looks like dry skin. Here's some lotion." I told her the Radiology doctor suspected Paget's Disease. She scoffed at the thought and said, "Come back if the lotion does not work after 30 days." Every 30 days, I returned to her complaining that my areola was getting worse. Each time, I was given a new lotion, liquid band-aid, valium, or nursing cups for inverted nipples. What I never received was a referral to a specialist.

It was a total of six months before I managed to maneuver my way to see a Dermatologist to look at my breast. The doctor was initially confused because as a dermatologist, she did not specialize in breasts. I begged her to just take a look. When she came to examine me, her immediate response was, "Dear God, you have cancer!" I cried tears of joy! Someone finally believed me. That momentous day was October 31, 2017. I was diagnosed with Paget's Disease of the Breast. I had my bilateral mastectomy on December 17, 2017.

You're Not Dead Yet... Get Up!

Turn on the Light
I learned that there is only a "Failure Freeway" if you choose to take that route. Don't consider a cancer diagnosis as a failure on your part. No one chooses cancer. We may be diagnosed, have surgeries and treatments, and endure years of uncertainty and fear, but I suggest you not choose to feel pity or failure.

No one wants to hear the words, "You have cancer". Unfortunately, many of us do. We must choose to take active action in our cancer fight. Allow yourself time to run through all your feelings. Set a short time period to contemplate and grieve; then get back up.

You have a lot of prime living to do. Life is too short and precious to squander too many days allowing any more darkness into your world. When you find yourself in the dark, turn on a light. The darker it is, the more effect even the tiniest light will have.

Healing Through Life's Gifts
My healing journey was first mental and spiritual before it was physical. When I heard my diagnosis, I already knew I had cancer roaming through my body.

My mental healing began well before any diagnosis. I needed to take ownership of what was happening. I refused to feel helpless and at the mercy of what I knew could kill me. My goal became to take control of my health in order to help my body fight more efficiently. I had to mentally choose that I would not make excuses for my health.

Spiritual healing has been ever-evolving. I have been thriving through my cancer journey in conjunction with my traumatic brain injury. This has made the search for a higher purpose and my need for legacy to drive me to be the best person I can be every day I have the blessing to wake up.

I have come to the realization that cancer didn't happen to me, it happened for me. I am a far better person today now that I have learned personally how priceless the gift of life is.

Physical healing is ongoing. Since my bilateral mastectomy, I have had eight more surgeries over a three-year period. Each surgery was challenging and came with its own complications, yet I am still here. I see the blessing as I push through the pain.

Every day, I find something else to be grateful for. Even with the pain, brain fog, and surgeries, I find my gifts.

Let It Go
My greatest achievement during the first two months after diagnosis was the writing and publishing of my second book, ***It's Not Luck - Overcoming You***. This accomplishment was significant for me because I wrote it as a guide and a motherly voice of reason for my children.

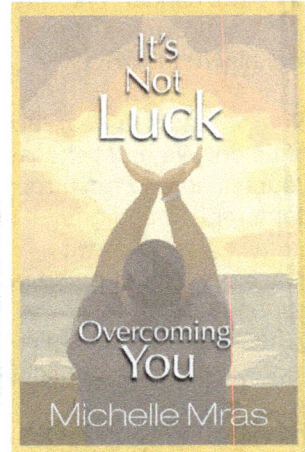

If I didn't survive the surgery or succumb to cancer, I wanted to be there for them to help them through their tough times and guide them when their inner critics stopped them from achieving their dreams and goals. After writing it, I decided the world also needed guidance through tough times and solid advice, so I published it and put it on Amazon.

My greatest lesson throughout this journey is:

"You are braver than you believe, stronger than you seem, and smarter than you think." - A.A. Milne

This cancer journey is not simple or easy. Every morning we must intentionally approach our day to live it fully and take time to enjoy the little moments. Those of us on this journey realize how precious those little moments are.

Another lesson learned is to forgive yourself and others. Holding a grudge or berating ourselves for what we could have done better or for precautions we could have taken to avoid our diagnosis is futile. There is no sense in wasting precious energy on non-productive thought processes. Let it go. If you find it difficult to let go, find a professional to help you talk through the process of how to let go of past pain.

You're Not Dead Yet... Get Up!

Live Life Unapologetically
My career did a complete shift with my breast cancer diagnosis. I became less afraid to be myself. If someone didn't like me, the thought no longer broke me. The squabbles and negativity in the world stopped depressing me. I have bigger problems in my world - being popular or developing an ulcer aren't on the list.

The courageous actions I take now are that I live unapologetically as me. I speak on hundreds of podcasts and internet television shows and write for magazines and blogs. I contribute to compilation books as well as write my own in order to help others remove the veil of inadequacies from their eyes.

I am an international speaker, award-winning author, narrator, actress, and award-winning coach. It is my mission in life to guide others to stop apologizing for what they aren't, embrace who they are, and be the best version of themselves every day... Unapologetically!

Four steps to live through difficult times:
1. You aren't alone. Find a positive tribe of thrivers to connect with.
2. Don't stop doing the things you love. Keep living.
3. Learn to be quiet through meditation. Every day, seek the lesson and joy in your journey. Calming your mind to allow it to process allows you to handle everyday stressors far easier.
4. Remember your family is experiencing their own stress about your diagnosis. Give them grace. They don't want to lose you.

Mending Broken Promises
Re-evaluate promises you made to yourself. A cancer diagnosis tends to help one see what truly matters in the big scheme of things. We don't need superficial relationships or activities that do not serve our well-being. Practicing self-love helps your mind, body, and soul come to a harmonious co-existence. The inner peace achieved through taking care of yourself is a precious gift to fuel the journey through the ups and downs of the emotional journey which is cancer.

These are the self-love acts I have incorporated into my life:
1. Meditating
2. Journaling
3. Exercising
4. Singing

You're Not Dead Yet... Get Up!

Be gentle to yourself. Cancer is no walk in the park. We have so much on our minds with the diagnosis along with the treatment plan. Get the thoughts out of your head about being selfish. Taking care of yourself first is far from selfish. Self-love is crucial throughout this journey.

It is how we fill our souls in order to mentally and physically battle this disease. This is how we calm our minds and soul so that we can be our unfrazzled selves. We have received a wake-up call to no longer take our lives for granted. Live unapologetically.

Cancer Affects the Family

My immediate family loved me through my fear and pain. They cared for me after each surgery and found food I could tolerate when it was difficult to eat. I could see the fear of losing me in their eyes. Their love for me kept me driven to keep fighting for my health and wellness. The entire family changed how they ate to match my nutritional needs. Personally, each of them took the news differently. My husband became very protective. He checked on my vitamin and caloric intake. He drove me to the doctor and attended every appointment.

Our daughter became concerned about how this cancer diagnosis would translate into her genetics. She became depressed, anxious, and less patient with people outside of our home. She took it upon herself to assume my role as the mother of the household. She organized the household cleaning schedule, made meal plans, and drove her brother to his activities. Our son was matter-a-fact about the diagnosis. He studied the types of cancer, prevention, and statistics of genetic links and would sit quietly near me and simply be with me.

You're Not Dead Yet... Get Up!

It was interesting to see the dynamics of how each of them showed their love and concern for my situation. My sisters and their families came to visit often, bringing food and taking my children on outings. My mother and brothers acted as if there was no diagnosis of cancer. If you don't acknowledge it out loud, it doesn't exist, right?

The response to my cancer diagnosis close friends was erratic. I am a military spouse, so my very close friends live in other states or countries. One friend came out for my bilateral mastectomy to support my husband during the surgery and my post-surgery.

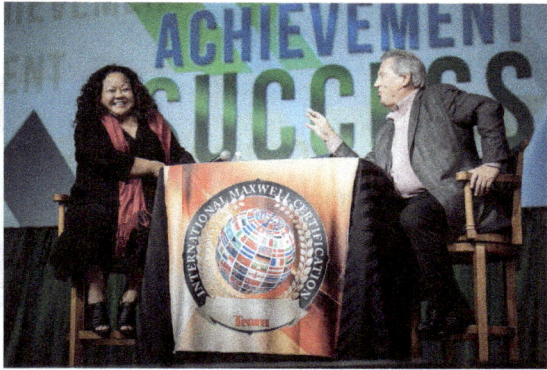

My next five closest friends waited until I was healed from my first surgery and all came to my home to have a mini-reunion. They came from as far away as Spain and Finland to be with me. Many of those in my own town seemed to simply avoid me, and a few individuals I considered acquaintances became very close friends.

Everyone processes grief differently. Give each person in your life grace regardless of how they respond to your diagnosis. I later spoke to a few past friends who abandoned me regarding why they stopped talking to me. One actually said he couldn't bear to watch a vibrant light go out. I found that interesting and selfish. Nevertheless, I forgave that person for being scared. God knows I was.

Chemo Buddies for Life

I did not have a cancer support system beyond my immediate family and a few very close friends. One in particular, Kim, had started her breast cancer journey two years prior to mine. She was a tremendous asset in my peer group. She kept me calm when I got lost in the medical jargon and medication names. She introduced me to the drain holders and the mastectomy pillow and how to find humor through the pain.

You're Not Dead Yet... Get Up!

Two years into my breast cancer journey, I met Tamera Hunter. She created a non-profit group called Chemo Buddies for Life or (CB4L.org). This is a place for us to bond and build friendships among people who understand all the feelings and fears we experience throughout the different aspects of the cancer journey. The group is for anyone who is in a cancer journey regardless of the type of cancer and anyone who loves them and wants a support group. I love the energy and the friendships I have built within the group. I wish I had had them when I was in the beginning stages of this journey. The group would have helped lessen my fears of the unknown.

Living and Leaving a Legacy

I live Unapologetically as a professional speaker spreading a message of inspiration and hope. I use my gifts with the written and spoken word to share the joy of living a life untethered by fear and the feeling of not being worthy. My legacy is shared within my professional talks, Denim

and Pearls podcast, Amplifluence podcast, a live-stream television show - Mental Shift on TNC and ZondraTV, multiple books, podcast interviews, magazine articles, children's book narration, singing, and movie roles.

If this breast cancer has taught me one thing, it is that life is too precious to play the game of life small. No one is promised tomorrow or the rest of today. Go do what you have dreamt of doing. Finish your life bucket list! Leave your mark on the world while you can, regardless of how small or big. When I was in the biggest battle in my cancer journey, I realized that I had the knowledge to share that I hadn't released from my mind. I began to write for my children to know our family history and what made me the person I am. I shared funny stories about the family. I wrote about the dreams I wanted to achieve.

You're Not Dead Yet... Get Up!

My husband read all of my journaled thoughts and said, "You should publish these to encourage others", so I did. My second book, "It's Not Luck - Overcoming You" was published within months of my diagnosis. Since then, I have contributed to ten other books, led an anthology, "Hold My Crown - Women of grit share stories of resilience", and narrated my first book which is based off my TEDx Talk, "Eat, Drink and Be Mary - A glimpse into a life well lived". What's your legacy? What do you want to be remembered for? Go out and make it so.

"Change is an emotional journey. It's not rainbows and butterflies in a field of daisies. Change is uncomfortable. It forces you to evaluate who you are. The beauty is in the possibilities!"
- Michelle Mras

Sometimes when you want to cry, it's just as easy to laugh and help others laugh with you. Shortly after my bilateral mastectomy, I got to go shopping for my artificial breasts. I'm brown-skinned, so I thought it would be funny to request white boobs. Honestly, I asked for rainbow-colored boobs They didn't have them. Anyway, we met friends for dinner at a local bar that night.

The artificial boobs were so new, and they looked great. I asked my friend sitting next to me, "Wanna see my boobs?" She gave me a puzzled look as I pulled a prosthetic boob out of my bra and put it in her hand. My husband looked in horror as she began to play with it like a stress ball. Everyone at the table proudly declared that they "felt my boob". It was a joyous moment that cut the undercurrent of "Michelle is very sick" out of the minds of those around me.

https://www.MichelleMras.com
(all social media links are on my website)

Book: Hold My Crown - Women of grit share stories of resilience (eBook)

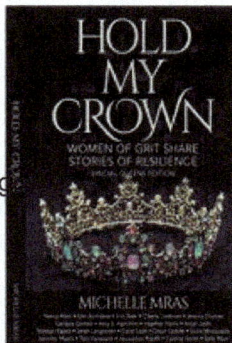

Complimentary digital book

MichelleMras.com

Chapter 14

You've Got This; It's Only a Duck!

Tamara L. Hunter

Tamara L. Hunter

First Global Next Impactor

Branson, Missouri, United States of America

SpeakerTamaraLHunter@gmail.com

> ❝
>
> *Never, never, never give up.*
>
> *Winston Churchill*

My name is Tamara L. Hunter. I am a motivational and inspirational speaker that believes there is healing through connections, and it is time to raise the frequency of the world through love. I believe it so much I have created two TV Shows, became a two-time best-selling author, built a global nonprofit support community, and became the "First Global Next Impactor."

I believe we are stronger together. I believe it so much, I co-wrote a song with Julie Christopher and Krystylle Richardson, "We Are The Ones." I also believe in humor, hope, heart, hugs, and a whole lot of love.

I would love to share this song with you! My teams created two versions for a thirty-six-hour live-streaming event, which I hosted called, "The Tour of Love." Here are two QR Codes to be able to watch them both. However, if they do not help or cheer you up, I dare you to say "humor, hope, heart, hugs, and a whole lot of love" multiple times. I know they help! They helped me; my hope is they will help you, too.

I am a top motivational, inspirational, personal and business development keynote speaker. The First Global Next Impactor. Founder of a global nonprofit online cancer and life-changing events support community CB4L.org. Creator, producer, and host of three TV shows that air on the e360TV Network. They are also found on ROKU, Amazon Fire TV, Apple TV, Android TV, plus all social media platforms. I am a coach, business consultant, magazine contributing columnist, and three-time best-selling author.

You've Got This; It's Only a Duck!

Not My First Rodeo!
Sometimes in life, we have opportunities to gain experience and lessons. When we continue to have the same opportunities, we start to wonder what we are missing.

Before my diagnosis, I had a life that would not fit here in only a paragraph or two. My life would be great material for at least one Lifetime Channel Movie or two or three.

I will share that when I had a "duck" I did not cry. When I went through testing and diagnosis for my nineteen-year-old daughter before mine, I cried and nearly had a breakdown. My brother, who was a survivor warrior, kept me together.

Life has a way to prepare us; little did I understand pre-2014, how much my life had been preparing me to face what would allow me to become a "Prize Fighter." Looking back now, I can see how important it was to have had the experiences I did before my diagnosis.

It's A Duck!
September 2014 was the month I received the call to have additional testing. I have been through this drill before, so I knew what it could mean.

My family had been through testing and diagnosis for my brother, my grandfather, and my daughter by the time my call came. When I received that call, I knew what I was most likely facing. I entered the testing room, and the tech knew me. She remembered me because she was the technician who helped me when my 19-year-old daughter went through testing and diagnosis. As I sat there, I was interested in the results more in a scientific way than an emotional way.

Of course, the medical professional could not tell me anything, yet she did say, "If it looks like a duck, acts like a duck, it most likely is a duck." As I left the medical clinic, I sat in my car alone realizing I was facing a duck.

Did I cry? No. I did not cry once. I knew from the moment that I "most likely" had a duck; the duck would become only one more chapter in my full book of life, and that I would survive and continue to my next chapter.

You've Got This; It's Only a Duck!

I did become a student of the treatments that were available. I started calling locally and nationally. The calls all started the same way, "Hello, I am calling to find out about and would state what it was then I would say, I have a duck." Oh, that phrase created incredibly fun phone calls. Later I would speak with one of the ladies that I first called. She told me she will forever remember the woman that had a duck.

I knew from the beginning my duck would only be with me for only a brief time. And it was.

They Are Real!
The dark nights of the soul are very real and do not let anyone tell you otherwise. With that said, do they need to overcome or overwhelm us? That is completely up to you.

In 2014 I did not know the technology that I now understand. I did not have or know how to use any type of facetime Apps or have software to visit with another remotely.

You see, I had gone underground for safety reasons years before, so I did not have any type of active social media or understanding of it. I had finally gotten a Facebook account yet kept it private. My purpose was to see my grandchildren's pictures even though they lived with me. Any grandparent will understand this desire, right?

When I became a "buddy" after my first treatment, I would reach out to my buddy and would visit via messenger. This contact became beyond healing. It truly became the shining light that got me through those long dark nights of the soul.

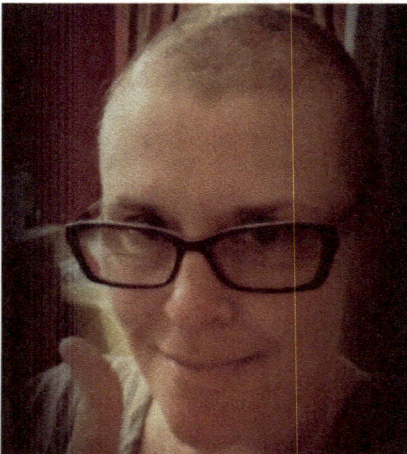

Are You OK?
As I had explained, I did not cry, and I was dealing with my duck. Little did I see that on the first day of treatment, I would experience a near-death moment that would change the course of my life going forward.

Being the Girl Scout that I am, I had multiple bags ready to go with me on my first day of treatment. When I arrived, the nurses had to seat me in the corner, so no one would trip on my "preparation."

You've Got This; It's Only a Duck!

Having the health history that I had, the doctors had decided to give me an extra dose of Benadryl to help ward off any allergic reactions. With five bags placed on "the pole", the first bag was administered. I fell asleep curled up into a ball under my comfy blanket.

Then I heard far away in a fog, "Are you ok?" I was in a very deep sleep. Again, I heard, "Are you ok?" I attempted to open my eyes and could not. Then I realized my face was on fire, and my throat was beginning to close. I knew I was not ok, yet I could not say anything. I do remember placing my hands at my throat.

The medical staff jumped into action, and I was saved. This experience would become an urban legion and would set me on the path I now walk. That voice was the daughter of the who became my original buddy. Our health journey together for the next two years translated into my life's work and mission to promote that there truly is "healing through connections."

Words Have Power!
Do you believe that there is power in words? And can you believe I am sharing this fact in a book devoted to those who are facing "those three words?" I thought I understood the power of words. In fact, I would have told you "pre-duck" that I understood their power and had them

mastered. Wow, when I found out how wrong I was, that was an extremely huge "aha moment" for me.

Let me explain further. We all have an internal computer, and our words are extremely important when dealing with it. For example, I used to say, "I will never" this or that. Do you know that my internal computer heard "I will" this or that? That was such a surprise to me. So, if I said, "I will never paint my room purple." My computer is hearing, "I will paint my room purple." This is huge stuff, right?

You've Got This; It's Only a Duck!

Coming from a family with our medical history, you would think I would be extra careful with my verbiage. I thought I was being, and I was not. Now I am. I realize that my internal computer can help determine my long-term health. It can help in multiple areas of my life.

If you get anything from my chapter, I hope you are getting this. Words have so much power over our overall health and much more. And the good news, in understanding this power, you can, too!

Social Media, Really?
You may find this funny; however, before 2014 I did not have any active social media accounts, and I was not interested in changing that. I said, "I will never be one of those people that share their lives through the internet." Yes, I did have safety concerns, too.

It has been a pure act of love and continues to be a learning experience for me to be as active as I am. I did have a computer, yet I used it to do family history and genealogy. I was a bit of a detective when it came to finding those who had passed.

Yet, to be using computers "socially" in the land of the living was something that I really had not found interest in pre-2014. It took having a "buddy" and then a calling to help those facing cancer and other life-changing events to change my mind.

Like I said before, you may find this funny, yet we all have our comfort zones, and social media was not my comfort zone although now I have grown to see the value that it offers and the internet shares. I can even say I am warming up to it. We can turn any opportunity into an area of growth.

Tamara's Game Closet
As a child, I loved board and card games. Now my grandchildren do, too. When I think back on my journey and growth, I can liken it to the games that you would find in my game closet.

You've Got This; It's Only a Duck!

1.   The Card Game Uno. I am going to add one word, "Mas." Uno mas means "One More." Sometimes we need to remember to not look beyond the moment. Take "Uno Mas" step at a time. Take "Uno Mas" moment at a time. Give yourself permission. It is OK!
2.   Battleship. When you play this game, you are looking to sink the other player's battleship. Need I say more?
3.   Poker. My mom taught me and my children poker. Every holiday we would get the cards and chips out and play. We did not play for money. My mom taught us that you can learn life skills through this game. And you can.
4.   Candyland. Instead of candy or sweets, think of self-care. It is the best game when you think this way.

My game closet is more of a metaphor, and my hope is that I have gotten you thinking. What four games would be in your closet and why?

Love Conquers All!
Life can be messy, and we will have times when we do life great and others when we do not. The best thing we can do for ourselves is to remember we are human and no human is perfect.

I believe in keeping it simple. Love heals. If we can remember to love others and to love ourselves, we will see miracles. How can I say this statement because I have witnessed true miracles? Love does conquer all.

Three Bald Men
December 10, 2014, was my first day of treatment. When I entered that treatment room, I was ready. I had my whole house decorated, bought, and wrapped all the presents, and sent out all the Christmas cards. I had visions of sitting with my family while I was in treatment through the holidays.My immediate family is small, and nearly all of them lived in my home at the time. At the time of my diagnosis, we were all unaware that my mom was also facing the same issue.

She was extremely sick, yet we believed it was pneumonia. Later we would find out she had Multiple Myeloma or bone marrow cancer. Due to pneumonia and my mom living in my home, I was isolated or in what I called to put into "solitary confinement." This was pre-COVID. I was unable to spend the holidays with my family. I spent it alone in my solitary room. Although I was not lonely, remember, I had a buddy.

You've Got This; It's Only a Duck!

Due to the isolation and to show support, the adult men in my family all shaved their heads. As I look back on it now, it was so sweet, yet I was unable to even see them face to face. I was behind closed doors. They did show me standing outside my sliding glass door that led to the backyard patio. There they were bald with huge smiles. So sweet.

My New Buddy
Other than my new buddy, pre-COVID, I could not find any online support, and I was not allowed out of my room. Thank goodness I had prepared as I did. My room became the only place in my home I was allowed to be for nearly a half year.

When I went through treatment, I was in isolation and had an unusually high amount of side effects; one of those side effects was chemo sores on my vocal cords. What happened? I lost my voice.

I did not do social media. I could not talk on the phone, and I could not spend time face-to-face with my family, yet I had a buddy and I could type. My buddy became my lifeline.

"Healing Through Connections"
I did not have a supportive community or family that I could see or speak with when I went through treatment. However, once I received a clean bill of

health and was able to start my new chapter, my doctors and nurses lobbied hard for me to create a situation that would empower, encourage, educate, and promote community for others facing a duck.

For over five years, I have dedicated my life to exactly what they requested me to do. I have used social media and the internet to create worldwide awareness, encourage others, educate, and promote the importance of community, and share that there is healing through connections.

You've Got This; It's Only a Duck!

Humor, hope, heart, hugs, and a whole lot of love really work. You can find out more at TamaraLHunter.com.

During COVID I would go live every morning as I went on my walk and encourage others to get up and go even if there was nowhere to go. During my Facebook Live, I would ask what is your theme song? Mine was, "Prize Fighter" by Trisha Yearwood. I played it every morning before I went outside to walk. I also did a bed check, "Have you made your bed? Make your bed and change the world." Or at least yours!

Always remember, you have the power, there are miracles, and there is healing in connections. You've got this… it is only a duck!

And, you, too, are a "Prize Fighter!"

Here is the QR code to listen to her song.

Social media information:
Facebook, Instagram, Twitter, LinkedIn, Clubhouse

Free Offer
I would love to give you, "The Celebration Journal; Full of Love, Health and Amazing Success." Go to www.CB4L.org and at the end of the page you can claim your free gift.

We have the power to change the direction of our world, yet we must do the work. And, we must do this work together. The time for change is now. We all know it. Join Me! Together we will change how we face cancer. Together we will experience healing in our families, our communities, our countries, and our world. Together we can raise the frequency through love. JOIN ME! www.tamara360.com

CONCLUSION

This is not a "Goodbye" but a time to push you over the edge. Live Life with intention because it will help you to live a fearless life. We are hoping that we touch lives in many ways. Do things in life that fulfill you.

How do you navigate life?
"If it doesn't feel right, it is not the right thing." Dr. B.

Why do something that makes you feel uncomfortable, frustrated, doubtful, and confused? Make a different decision.

Everyone needs someone, especially for inspiration or to gain ideas on how to move forward in life. Learn to play the game of life. Treat life like a journey so explore it. Making a wrong decision means nothing if you are staying stuck; that doesn't make sense. Everything you experience in life is preparing you for something bigger than you can imagine. Allow failure to be your friend. When something goes wrong, it is time to learn something new about yourself. Recognize, accept, and shift the paradigm. When there are moments of uncertainty and when things are not going well, this means it is time to take another step or move in a different direction. Nobody makes it alone so find your community and support, a spiritual practice that nurtures the essence of you.

Learn to love "thyself". If you love yourself, you will love those around you. You will have something better to offer to humankind. Use love as a tool of service. If you don't know what to do, be still. The answer will come during those moments of silence. You will know the right choice for you. You are nothing if you feel lost and if you don't know "thyself". If you hit a dead end, it is time to move on to another path and go in a different direction. Life always whispers, and when you are in a dark place, life is now screaming to tell you it is time to get out. Surrendering is a way to act with responsibility to find solutions and an exit from your dark moments.

CONCLUSION

Someone out there has the light to help you get through your difficult time. We hope we are the light that is shining on your path and way out.

You must also ask, what is this challenge teaching me? For a moment stop pointing the finger and blaming others; take a new action. Your number one job now is to reflect on what you desire. If you are out of sync, it is time to line yourself up with life which will open doors. Life is every breath you take and a moment to live life fully. Live to the fullest! Life is always speaking to you through events and circumstances. Pay attention. Forgive yourself and others to become who you are meant to be. It might be time to let go of the past. What happened in the past will never change, but you must fast forward to regain your POWER. Move on. This is not easy but necessary to be able to live in peace and freedom. Liberate yourself from the past. Choose PEACE which leads to a sense of FREEDOM—your bridge to YOU!

Now DARE to BE YOU! People may not like you or accept you, but I am here to tell you that you matter, too. If you want to take a vacation, do it! You might think you don't have money or don't have anyone to come with you. You have to figure it out and just do it. You might want a relationship and might not feel worthy. Your breast or nipples don't define you if you had a double mastectomy. Your heart and attitude will define you.

Don't allow obstacles or excuses to get in the way of achieving your dream or doing what you truly desire. Remember to connect with all the co-authors in this book. You can connect with me via the Facebook community platform. Connect with people until you fill your cup, and it flows over onto others who need you. Then go and fill it up again–again until we leave this planet.

CONCLUSION

Keep an eye out for my next book, "Sexy After Cancer: Nipples nor Scars Don't Define You!"

So how do you live a life of substance? Figure out your boundaries, change the way you look at things, and identify what you really desire in life. Explore how to play the game of life, and most importantly DARE to BE YOU! Stop making excuses.

William Ernest Henley said, "You are the master of your fate and the captain of your soul"! Take charge of your destiny. So you can be proud and overflow in life without ego but full of gratitude and freedom to be who you want to be. Be proud of living and leave a legacy for generations to come.

I will now ask **the Bigger Questions.**

Answer this question: **Who am I? And What do I want?**

My answer is the following:
I am God's child and a spiritual being living to have a human experience. All that is possible is possible for me. I have a vision and direction for my life. I am in the driver's seat of my own life. Tomorrow if I leave this world, I feel content that I was who I dared to be, which is exceptional, extraordinary, and unforgettable. **Be Courageous! DARE to BE YOU!**